F.A.S.T.

Families-Always-Stronger-Together

A Holistic Guide
For The Restoration
Of Youth And Parents

By *Trillazan*

Copyright © 2017 by Trillazan Cole

F.A.S.T. — Families-Always-Stronger-Together:
A Holistic Guide For The Restoration Of Youth And Parents

Author: Trillazan Trailblazer

Editor: Michael T. Petro, Jr.
PetroPublications.com

Published in the United States of America
Published by Petro Publications

Front & Back Cover Photos:
Copyright © by Trillazan Cole

ISBN-10: 0-9650411-7-4

ISBN-13: 978-0-9650411-7-1

Dedication

This book is dedicated to all youths, parents, counselors, and all other concerned individuals who are working to restore the integrity of the family in every community across the globe that has suffered any form of spiritual or emotional deterioration!

Table Of Contents

Preface

There has been a systematic dismantling of honest-to-goodness value across the board. Products and services have become perfunctory and bland. Much of our religious practice has also developed into the same cookie-cutter uniformity Sunday after mundane Sunday from across town and across the country. Our law enforcement, courts and correctional institutions operate hand in hand as a business enterprise whose stock and trade are the people and residents within the community. The education system does more to indoctrinate than educate. On and on it goes!

The cornerstone of all these societal constructs is the family. Family is made up of people in homes and neighborhoods; people who shop at the corner store and attend church and school in the community.

There is a growing concern in some circles about the erosion of family and moral descent in the country and around the world.

Our world, nations, states, cities, neighborhoods, and families of origin are all cut from the same cloth. The family has been under attack for a long time. Most fail to see or realize that there has been a war declared on the family. Many of the resulting ills presented in modern society have come about as a direct result of families having no real conception of just how much they are being bombarded into an unrecognizable entity. Therefore, family does not defend itself.

If we are wise, we must ask ourselves at least a few questions: From where is this assault emanating? What can I do as a parent or community leader to regain lost ground? What can I do to make the world better for my children and grandchildren? There are many more questions to ponder. A wise person once said, *"As the family goes, so goes the nation."*

In this book you will see compelling truths regarding family, community and other societal constructs. Answers to these and other questions are discussed, along with positive, ethically principled directions to help restore both the family and the community.

Chapter One

Education is Key

As I walked up to the elementary school where I facilitated a Tobacco Education and Prevention Workshop, I couldn't help but notice the police cars and an ambulance in front of the main entrance. I wondered what had happened! Maybe one of the children got hurt in gym class or, you know kids, they probably were fighting again and somebody got more than they gave in the fine art of pugilism. With the concrete foundation, many of the playgrounds are built on, I supposed that maybe somebody fell at play and an image of a kid with head gashes from falling off of the jungle gym popped into my mind. I even thought that perhaps a teacher had taken seriously ill. And I can't say that the school shootings that we hear about far too often never crossed my mind either, and I wondered if something like that was going on. Just in the seconds it took for me to walk from my car up to the door so many possibilities skipped as effortlessly as a fresh gazelle through my mind. However, there was nowhere near the amount of law enforcement presence there to indicate that shootings were the case, but I still wondered what could have happened.

It was a very nice, sunny day in this quiet neighborhood with the well-painted homes and their perfectly manicured lawns. It must have been about 75 degrees outside on this early after-noon. I had worn my light blue shirt with the short sleeves today because the forecast was sunny and 83 degrees. My dark blue tie with the light stripes went well with that shirt and my dark blue Dockers slacks. I always went to school looking like a teacher because you've got to look the part to be the part. Kids are keen; if they see an area or something about you to ridicule, get ready cause you're going to get it — and how! As I said, I wanted to be effective as a teacher so I dressed appropriately. I often marveled at just how beautiful this school was; it reminded me more of a modern mansion in some ways than a school. I really thought that the circle through driveway was a very nice touch and added a home-like quality to this school that was very unique and just nice — very nice!

In any event, I had work to do as a facilitator of the Tobacco Education and Prevention Program for the kids in grades five through eight, so I rang the bell and once the receptionist buzzed me in, I walked into the school's front entrance. It was my job to teach kids how to say *"No"* to the onset of tobacco use:

"Tobacco use is the primary cause of preventable death in the United States. It accounts for more than 440,000 deaths per year, more than alcohol, cocaine, crack, heroin, homicide, suicide, car crashes, fire and HIV/AIDS combined. At least 2,000 U.S. children and adolescents begin tobacco use each day. Of these, nearly 500 will die in adulthood from tobacco-related diseases, primarily heart disease and atherosclerosis, cancers and chronic obstructive lung disease."

These were the findings of Steven Sussman; a Southern California professor and developer of the Youth Tobacco Education and Prevention Program that I taught in this school system. This information is what I began each new class with in order to grab the attention of the students; it never failed to spark conversation. Being in a school setting as a teacher was truly interesting in many ways; first I reflected on my own school-age children who are involved in various activities at their school. I wondered if school is for them as it was for me when I was growing up in public school, or is it more like it is here? Are there the same types of peer pressures and curriculum challenges that I faced? Oh boy! Some subjects I just hated when I was in school, such as math and history. Yuck! All of a sudden for some reason I got the taste of lima beans in my mouth just thinking about that, but let's move on.

As I look back today, I wish that I had held a love for those subjects then because I sure do need them now. I also wondered if my children face daily social challenges similar to what my students face here in this school system about 30 miles from where we live. To be perfectly honest, school is rather different now than it was when I was a grade school student, and I don't mean different as in better or simply distinctive. I teach in many different schools. During a typical day I am in three to four different schools. School is nothing like what I remember as a grade school student here in Northeast Ohio 40 years ago.

There are students in my classes who demonstrate initiative and a desire to learn; possessing the spark of hope of becoming what their dreams tell them that they can become. I see young people who have true intelligence and the wherewithal to get their necessaries done; individuals who will undoubtedly acquire the tools required to develop successful futures. I have been so impressed by the creativity and spontaneity that today's young people possess. Quick wit is what momma used to call it when people catch on fast. That's it, they have quick wit! They just seem to have a special instinct.

The vast majority of my students however reflected something that on the surface appears much less praiseworthy. I saw individuals who did not mind and even seemed to enjoy the prospect of becoming cooperative underclass citizens in a society which only values money and conformity. Far too many of my students demonstrated apathy and indifference to future successes or failings as it related to these issues; they just didn't seem to care either way. It was discomforting and very upsetting to say the least to see young people, the future of our nation, demonstrating total disregard for their education, each other, and authority. Most distressingly they had no regard for themselves. It's as if they didn't care about or want anything that had a positive value in their future. What could be a possible explanation for conduct of such a perplexing brand?

In the upcoming chapters we will search out some possibilities that may answer this and other questions regarding today's youth and how we have come to such a crossroad. I will continue to share personal experience and researched information in my quest for answers. It is my hope that together we will break through some longstanding myths and tear down barriers that separate one generation from another. We will also have an opportunity to consider the mirror of truth, truths that shaped us individually and as a nation. Such truths may have a bearing on today's youth and the difficulties they face.

We will ask ourselves if we are at present where we as parents and community leaders should be? To accurately lead we must, out of necessity, overcome the very things we seek to have our youth avoid. Each generation builds on the shoulders of their forerunners. We must be all that we can be in order that our youth can develop fully into the glorious image they were intended to become with the aid of our example and testimony.

During my formative years, as kids we dreamed of becoming great leaders of influence and integrity. We saw Martin Luther King, Jr. and Malcolm X speak, and we saw James Brown perform. James Brown came from a past filled with hardship to later become the "godfather of soul." He was indeed super "bad." (Bad meant good or something like that back then and he was super at it.)

I always admired Texas Senator and U.S. Representative Barbara Jordan! My-oh-my, that lady spoke like a mighty cherub sent to declare God's edict. It seemed like she received the words to say directly from God Himself. Her words were filled with power and direction. She was the first African American elected to the Texas Senate since Reconstruction. Many of my peers admired great leaders as well and felt a sense of responsibility to carry on with the struggle of an oppressed people striving to accomplish unrealized liberty and true freedom.

We trusted in God and the strength of unity. It was all *"right on and bloods thicker than the mud."* We called each other brother or sister; the whole community was family in an altruistic sense. Remember daddy and granddaddy, mama and grandma, Uncle Buddy and all of us kids being at the house on a regular basis? Remember the love and respect we had for each other? As children, even if we did not like or agree with what our elders told us to do or not to do, we respectfully obeyed them. By contrast just the other day I witnessed a calamity, an unfortunate incident between two daughters and their mother. The girls live with their mother; a single mom. This woman is a good friend of mine who I happen to be visiting at the time when her two daughters, 16 and 19 years old, began punching, cursing, and wrestling with their mother simply because mom had picked up their mess from her living room and placed it in the girl's room. The girls even went to the extreme of going to the kitchen and got knives and launched furious threats. I attempted to break this fight apart and I got cussed out too. All this happened because the girls didn't want to have to be responsible for their own mess. They wanted the untidy, messy, pile of clutter that they themselves created, to remain in the living room and not in their own room where they could clean it up or live with it. It was a shocking and very disturbing occurrence.

I have family down in Cincinnati, Ohio who we visited as kids at least two or three times a year. We never wanted to leave them because the bond was, and remains, so strong; it's like a spiritual tie, a feeling of belongingness and accountability that cannot be denied or resisted. There is nothing quite as satisfying as knowing where you belong and being there.

Remember when Mr. Wilson down the street told you that he was watching you? If you got out of line he would grab you by the arm and take you home and he told on you to your parents; then you really got it! Back then, in most cases it was not a perverted or a bad thing for your neighbor to have his or her eye on you; people looked out for each other in the neighborhoods then. We talked to each other and it was not uncommon to have your neighbor visit you in your home. It was very rare to see the type of character twisting that is so prevalent today. Nowadays we don't even know our next door neighbors name and it's rare if we even say *"Hello"* to each other.

Sidebar: As kids we got to stay outside and play till momma called "Time to come in," or maybe it was when the street lights came on. Whichever came first, you just knew it was time to come home!

When we were out of doors playing, ma always called the eldest siblings name first when it became time to come in for the night. She followed his name with *"yawl."* Yawl is the short version of *"you all."* It sounded something like this: Ma called out, *"Randy!"* Randy yelled back from the ball field, *"Huh!"* Ma yelled back again: *"Yawl come on in the house now; it's gettin dark."* Randy would say, *"OK!"* Then Randy told all the rest of us, *"Mama said we gotta come in,"* and so we went.

You were never too far away that you couldn't hear momma's voice. Remember when you could get a full bag of candy for a dime at Mrs. Bea's corner store? Mrs. Bea knew your parents as well as everyone else in the neighborhood because at some point everybody went to her store to buy odds and ends. Therefore, you certainly knew better than to steal anything or act out in her store. It never occurred to you to do such a thing anyway because your mom and dad taught you better. You believed them, you respected them, you honored your mom and dad and it just felt right; there was order to life.

Thinking back on those days brings a smile to my face. That's how it was for many families then as parents raised children in the lower middleclass neighborhoods of Ohio's Northeast back in the 1950s and 1960s. For the most part we got along swell.

I just had my 40th class reunion last year. Forty years, is that so far removed from today? Is that really that long ago that we have truly lost sight of the values of that era? Gee-whiz, time is moving so very fast. It's like if time were measured in fluid units we could fit two gallons of living and learning into what once only held a quart. Likewise, it seems that the distance between January and December has shortened to only five months. Such a large amount of information dissemination, movement, and focus shifting is taking place at such a rapid pace that it is difficult to maintain a line of sight on truth and fiction, real or unreal, appropriate or inappropriate.

Formerly young people were more apprehensive about peculiar adults than adults being apprehensive about peculiar youths. There used to be an old man or old woman in every neighborhood who all the kids thought was strange and we had stories whether real or fancied about their weirdness, like the old man with the snow shovel in the *Home Alone* movie.

Think about this for a moment: would you have some anxiety if you were walking down the street alone and four teenage urban or suburban youths (male and/or female) were walking toward you at about 9:00 p.m. on a summer evening? Think about the stories you've heard or read. I believe I would think about what counter measures I would need to take if anything were to jump off as I walked closer to the approaching group of youths. I think I would be sizing up the situation and wondering if I was in some kind of state of affairs which would require me to cross the street or turn around. If I did or not, I suppose I would think about it.

Allow me, if you will, to share this account of what happened the other day as I walked down a street in my hometown. Rain was now falling lightly after a heavy storm had passed through. People had begun to come back outside and move about after the rain subsided. It was still grey outside but the darker, more threatening clouds were giving way to those less ominous. Leaves and grass still soaking wet and the sidewalk damp, I began walking to a friend's home that lived several blocks away. As I reached a long stretch of sidewalk I looked 30 yards ahead and saw four teenage girls walking towards me.

As cars came down the street hitting the puddles near the rain water runoff areas of the curb, splashes of water thundered forcefully onto the sidewalk. When car tires hit the puddles near me the water splashed up and would dampen the leg of my Levi's. As the young girls got closer I moved to the curb, you know, as the gentlemanly thing to do to allow them to pass by securely. Well, the teenagers, about junior high school-age, flanked each other as they were close to passing me. To my surprise the one nearest to me made a resolute effort to not give any space for me to stay on the sidewalk by separating from the other girls as wide as possible. At the moment of passing she put her hands on her hips to form an elbow shoulder thumping maneuver and she actually bumped me as if to attempt to force me into the street. I turned as they had passed to look back at the youths, and they all continued walking without an *"excuse me"* or anything; they just kept right on "walkin and talkin." How unsettling is that?

I still say *"Yes ma'am"* and *"Yes sir"* to my elders as respectful terms. I also help my parents with whatever I can help with because it's appropriate and the right thing to do. I am blessed to still have both parents and I recognize it as such; it is indeed a blessing! Is honoring your elders, as we used to call it, now out dated or does it only apply to one's own parents, not the general public? I don't know; I have seen youngsters stand toe-to-toe cussing their parents in public and throwing up their fists as if to say "*Let's get it on,*" TO THEIR OWN MOM OR DAD!

There was a news story not long ago about a young man who was living with his mother. The story describes an incident in which the young man punched his mother in the head, knocking her down the basement stairs, breaking her neck as she fell to the bottom of the steps. Wow! What's up with that?

Oh yeah, as I was saying about the school, I rang the bell and the office receptionist spoke through the intercom asking, "*Who is it?*" She buzzed me in after I was identified. Upon entering the school and signing in at the front office and noticing that all seemed normal, I went down the hall to prepare for my class of fifth graders.

Typically, I would knock on the door to let the regular teacher know that I was there to begin the workshop, and he or she would finish what they were doing and tell the students to get out their books for my class. So as I knocked I looked in through the glass door and noticed all the students were missing and an emergency medical team was in the classroom attending the teacher as she sat in a wheelchair. Suddenly from another door across the hall abruptly there appeared an obviously heated police officer escorting in handcuffs a young African American male about 10 to 12 years old out of the school.

I was flabbergasted at the realization that it was one of the students that I had in my class. What could he have done that he was getting arrested? What was it that made that cop so angry? Suddenly things were moving a lot faster, the medical team then wheeled the teacher past me as I stood there in the hall, bewildered. I could see she was in great pain, but what had happened? I knew her well but she uttered not one word to me when they rolled her by. She appeared put away by the pain she was experiencing.

Suddenly, uneasy, I turned, measuring my steps as I headed back to the office to ask where my class of students were and what was going on, and what had happened to the teacher, and why all the police? I was puzzled by the events unfolding before me. Just then through the opposite door of the classroom came the students with a substitute teacher. The students were agitated as the substitute teacher yelled *"Everyone to your seats, quiet down!"* Needless to say, at this point I've got a little adrenaline pumping and my antenna is up, gauging for the slightest indication of what had happened. After a few pensive moments in the classroom with the students I told them to get their books out so we could begin, as they did so I asked in a sort of matter-of-fact way what had happened to your regular teacher. What resounded from the entire class, as if they couldn't wait to tell me, was a collective *"He beat her up! He beat her up,"* they joyfully exclaimed!

The crescendo of conversation became very noisome with haste. And I had to take command of the situation quickly because it was getting out of hand with the cross talking and jubilant chatter. Once I could manage through the noise it began to become clear that the young student who the angry police officer took out of the school had caused the teacher to twist her ankle during a scuffle between her and him. The police were taking him to juvenile detention while she was on her way to the emergency room for x-rays.

A fifth-grade student physically fighting his teacher and obviously getting the better of her! Does that sentence sound like something here is wide off the beam, out of place, inappropriate, or just plain wrong? I'll answer that one myself, *"YES!"* And this type of occurrence is far more frequent than one would suppose.

I cannot think of anything more incorrect or perverted as the student taking charge of the teacher or as in the case of my friend and her two daughters, the child usurping authority over the parent. The team running the coach or the mouse chasing the cat! Upside down, ain't it? Where did an authority transfer or a shift in weight take place? Is there a time or incident we can point to where parents or leaders capitulated, forfeited, or surrendered commanding influence over our youth?

As I stated earlier, this school building where I was teaching when this particular incident took place was very nice; it was only two years old and very pleasant to be inside this structure. It had the ambiance of a fine home or cathedral outwardly, however inside there was not as much illumination as outwardly it may have appeared.

There was it seemed, something less praiseworthy going on in the building than the praiseworthiness of the building itself. The heart of any school is its students; the learning that takes place within the walls of the learning institution is its heartbeat. This was a target school specifically designed for students in grades three through eight. It had a new computer lab. It also had 42 inch HD TV screens in nearly every classroom for school information to be easily reviewed, or for special programming to be taken in by the students without having to move them from room to room.

Sidebar: *By contrast, I recall when I was in grade school our teacher rolling out the big 25-inch, 70-pound TV set on the five foot high stand. Two or three classrooms assembled in the hallway to view the supposed landing of the Apollo space craft, the president's speech, or some other national event or* *educational activity. When we were fortunate enough to get a movie, one of the students went to get the old reel-to-reel projector from the classroom that had it last. When the projector was rolled into our room, the painstaking process of rewinding the huge reel of film and threading the projector commenced. Invariably once you got to the good part of the movie the tape would break and the rethreading process began anew. Either the tape was reparable or we never saw the end of the movie.*

My point is simply this: technology is much greater today than it was just a few short years ago, but do we appreciate it? Are the fullest benefits of it being realized? Technology is to be used for the betterment of humanity; in most respects, I would say that it is but as with anything else, there are two sides to every story. For example, during the course of my computer training class at which I taught individuals how to operate a PC and navigate through the Internet, I found it challenging to keep some of the boys off of the porn sights whenever I left the room.

It's the heart of an individual which determines how he or she will utilize anything, including technology. In my opinion, the eyes of mankind's spirit have been slowly closing for many years to the extent that not much light gets through our collective spiritual cornea nowadays. Subsequently the heart of mankind grows colder, harder, and darker with each subsequent generation.

Returning to the present-day school in question, the brand-new library wing of this school was filled with all types of information dispensing equipment, history books, again HD TV's, computers, new tables and chairs, and it was beautifully carpeted, and it even had a glass dome ceiling. The students in the school were predominantly African American, maybe 80 or 90%. As far as the staff goes, the principal and community and family liaison were also African American, but the remainder of the staff was not.

Sidebar: *Have you ever noticed some of the movies that have an African American star with the big name only to find out he or she is just about the only African American in the entire picture? Hmmm! Interesting!*

What I can recall regarding the remaining staff was that they were maybe 95% Caucasian and almost all women! Once again, hmmm! It's just an observation, that's all. The only other men in the school that I saw were the gym teacher, a very tall white man who had played college basketball. He was a very good teacher and had great rapport with his students. He and I often talked about the Cleveland Cavaliers and Lebron James while we waited for class to begin. The security officer was an African American man, and then of course there was me. I never thought anything much about it at the time; there being so few men, especially African American men, in the building. It's just sort of interesting; one of those things that make you go, *"Hmmm!"*

Seeing as how roughly 80 to 90% of the student body was African American, many of which were boys, caused me to speculate as to why there were so few African American teachers, and of the total, why so few males? Were African American's truly less qualified or unqualified altogether to teach? Did men not apply for such positions? The students frequently presented behavior issues such as aggression or disassociation and disregard for authority figures. Many students seemingly had little esteem for their largely white female faculty. Not to suggest that if the racial or gender composition of the faculty were made up differently they would receive a better or different response from the students; it's just an interesting observation.

I also facilitated the Tobacco Education and Prevention Workshop in grades six through eight as well as these fifth-grade classes. Unfortunately, my experiences were just as unsettling in each of the other grade levels in regard to student apathy. It was even more atypical to have students prepared with pens or pencils, although I provided pencils and pens myself nearly each day; however, consistently the next day students had none, as Mr. Spock of *Star Trek* would say, *"Fascinating!"*

It was equally common finding students with a desire to learn as it was to find the apathetic. It was as if, for the most part, the uninterested students did not bother themselves with the small stuff like reading, writing, and math. They certainly did not bother in my class; those things interfered with the more important pursuits like learning the lyrics of the latest rap song and most importantly, how to beat the most challenging video games like Grand Theft Auto. They understood these topics with great clarity and precision. In this particular game, Grand Theft Auto, you steal cars and run over pedestrians while carrying out nefarious schemes assigned by the over boss.

While in the schools I did note some very good concerned and caring teachers, but sad to say it appeared that many of the teachers didn't concern themselves much about the student's education either. I know, I know, and before you jump on me for saying that teachers don't care, I'm not saying that at all. From my perspective, many teachers appeared exhausted and out of control as they desperately alternated between teachers to judicial court judge, from warden to court jester. The class seemed more in command than the teachers. I am certain that the teachers care a great deal about their work, but at times may become overwhelmed. I wondered, was this a circumstance that was true elsewhere or everywhere?

As my duties took me to additional schools in the public as well as private school systems, I became acutely aware that something was seriously afoot here. Things had certainly changed since I was a student in the public school system. Large numbers of students presented the appearance of being hopeless and helpless as it related to genuine learning. There appeared more of a punitive or disciplinary system underway than an authentic educational system. The school staff offered little or no resistance to the unmanageable juggernaut of youthful indifference set before them. The staff, while working with great fervor, somehow looked like they were frantically trying to catch water in their hand. Maybe it was just that the resistance offered by staff amounted to that of a thimble being scooped out of the ocean, which largely went undetected as classroom size and the numbers of disorderly youth grows exponentially.

Too often what we have is impotent attempts by teachers to impart useful information between the *"go to the offices,"* the *"sit downs,"* the *"stop thats"* and the ever present *"be quiets"* to scores of students who have heard it all so many times before that they don't seem to hear those commands anymore. Observing this resembles a skydiver whose chute won't open as he flounders, plummeting to the Earth with the parachute twisted and tangled while everyone watches in horror from the ground, helpless to offer any assistance.

In many instances, we as teachers are in deep water up to our necks and it won't take much more to drown us. Several tragedies are clearly painted in this picture, one being the predicament of the teacher and another is that of the students who will follow the teacher in a like manner, hitting the ground or drowning if real solutions are not reached soon. Drowning and falling are both time sensitive events, which require emergency responses. While there are excellent teachers who present clear, concise, and resolute lessons to their classes — and many students flourish under their tutelage — far too many students are resistant to becoming educated in the "unimportant" subjects like reading, writing and math. These subjects appear to interfere with the weightier subjects we just talked about in a preceding paragraph.

I know people who have been in prison before, as I am sure many of us do. I myself have spent several weeks in jail. For those of you who have never been imprisoned, understand one thing, it is a very controlled environment, so don't make plans to go there! If you think that you are not treated with much respect now, only imagine what it would be like in an atmosphere in which you are simply another number among many numbers to the establishment — and prey to other inmates.

I have seen how society at large functions for those of us who are considered free citizens also. I have seen religious organiza-tions whose priorities lay more along the lines of legalism where observance of the church or denominational rules and policies take precedence over salvation, love, compassion, and worship. The revolving door of our court system, which has more of a vested interest in keeping one involved in the system than having one become a free, law-abiding individual, thus appear-ing to be a snare which is set in place to capture and cling to a person rather than set him on a correct path to true citizenship.

I have watched business practices of self-styled free enterprise capitalism as well. Observance of these community constructs begs these simple questions: Are our schools simply microcosms of the larger community as a whole? Could the ills I have just described regarding what is going on in the schools have its roots in other segments of society? Could it be that authoritarian figures primarily concern themselves with punitive measures and manipulation of youthful minds, not real education that cultivates creativity and balance? Could it be that more money, vigor and time are spent on attempts at indoctrination, control, and behavior modification, instead of fostering learning and imagination? Are our inner city schools more closely aligned with correctional institutions than that of true educational institutions?

If indeed there is any factual basis for these questions being answered affirmatively — and I believe there is — and it's not simply a whimsical hypothesis on my part, we need to ask ourselves this follow up question: Have the youth of today recognized that much of what we instruct them in is to meet our own ends and to bring them into failing economic, cultural, educational, religious and correctional systems? Could it be that they are rebelling against this? Could it be that our youth see the fallacy of the constructs of previous generations that we ourselves cannot see? Even if they have only a secondary understanding or just a subconscious level of knowing that they are being played somehow, how would they react? How would you react?

The Manual says that we would be set free by knowing the truth. Truth is sometimes elusive and difficult to know, particularly when truth is looking back at you from the mirror, yet our recognition is simply the reflection of our own visage and we fail to truly see ourselves in totality. But as a society, who are we really and what have we become must be the questions we ask of ourselves?

Recognition and acknowledgement of truth is a vital factor in living effectively. However, are we capable of receiving realities that come from unfamiliar voices or faces? The living Manual says that the word of God is like a mirror and if we look intently into it, we see ourselves as we truly are. When you look into the mirror of God's word what do you see? Do we even truly look into this mirror? How many of us realize that our youth are simply mirrors of previous generations? I can only answer for myself. You must answer for yourself. Answers to these and other questions are central to the focus of this book and will be examined more carefully in upcoming pages. I submit to you that this generation of young people did not simply become disinterested apart from our cooperation or encouragement to wonder from our path. We have partnered with our youth to bring about what we see today. Whether good or not so good, preceding generations are equally, if not more so, responsible for the present state of affairs with today's youth.

Chapter Two

Dedication to Communication

Consistency of message is a vital part of any communication. How is it then, that the messages being sent to our youth are so diverse? Some examples of the dissimilarity of signals would be how we as parents take our children to church for worship; that is, of the percentage of us that attend. The contrast of our church life from our home life many times is so dissimilar that it can be very confusing to the youth in and around our homes.

According to an online article at Churchleaders.com,[1] based on head counts the rate of church attendance in America is less than half of the 40% pollsters have reported. A study published in 2005 in *The Journal for the Scientific Study of Religion* found that the actual number of people worshipping each week is about 52 million. This figure represents a mere 17.7% of the American population, and not the 132 million, or 40%, reported by pollsters. The study consisted of American adults who attend church in a given weekend, and did not include attendance for a special event such as a wedding or a funeral. The study was conducted by sociologists C. Kirk Hadaway and Penny Long Marler, both of whom have an established reputation for scholarly research on the church, and this adds credibility to their finding.

There is a veritable smorgasbord of religions to choose from, ranging from the most pious, devout God-fearing belief, all the way down the to the subbasement level of Satan worship. Virtually anything you want is available, and everything is subject to one's own interpretation. We range from 100% committed to loose association as worshipers. We present to other parishioners a form of piety that is unrecognizable to our children in our home life with our families and neighbors, all the while our children look on with amazement, attempting to figure it all out. Our children overhear our telephone conversations with our friends in which we talk maliciously about the next-door neighbor, or sister so-and-so, who we just left at church. We tell the kids *"Be kind and truthful cause Santa knows if you've been bad or good, so you better be good for goodness sake."* And, *"Do what I tell you, not what you see me do!"*

Sidebar: *Among the 10 Commandments we find the following statement contained within the 2nd Commandment: "for I the Lord thy God am a jealous God, visiting the iniquity of the fathers upon the children unto the third and fourth generation of them that hate Me; And shewing mercy unto thousands of them that love Me, and keep My commandments." (King James Version: Exodus 20) What we do as adults does affect our youth!*

Our youth see the type of television programming we watch and the undeserved advantage we take of others. Our kids know of our business practices as well as the different ways in which we relate to our community.

For instance; we sometimes bring home items from work and share them freely with our family as if it's just a benefit of working at the company. HELLO! Your kids know you stole it. When we get angry the words that come from our sanctified mouths are enough to win first prize in a cussing contest. All the while at church we are shouting and dancing out of our cloths, speaking in tongues and "prophelying:" *"Thank you Jesus I'm so happy to be saved and sanctified and filled with the precious gift of the Holy Ghost, Hallelujah Gods not done with me yet, I'm a work in progress and He understands, after all He made me this way and I'm waiting for my change to come, blessed be the name of the Lord"* is how we rationalize staying in this system of sameness. All through the Bible we are called to change, far too many appear more comfortable unchanged.

Not to mention the premarital, extramarital and the on the down low sex, OK! These things are pure confusion and they leave a question mark in the unbeliever's mind and certainly leaves question marks in the minds of our youth. What would a child think when brother so-and-so spends the night in their mom's room but at church they are just casual acquaintances?

By contrast do our young see us demonstrate real love and compassion toward the fatherless, orphans or the poor? What about true repentance and hearts poured out to God, at home not just when others see us, others we want to impress with our religious piety? What is our prayer life like in front of our kids? How much time would your family say that you spend reading your Bible? Can they say my folks spend daily time in the word and share Gods truths with me consistently in word and deed? Actually, can our youth say with confidence that their parents communicate using encouraging expressions of affirmation towards them most of the time — at least sometimes? Or do we just focus on what they do wrong? Do we put into practice the things we say we believe and teach them diligently to our youth?

Am I consistent as a parent to do what I say for my family or my community? Am I a giver or a taker? How would those who know us best answer these questions about us? I admit I have some work to do. Our youth may know us best and they are watching, learning and growing into adulthood based largely on what they learn from us either intentionally or unintentionally. Whether we admit it or not, we are their most prominent role models. How would they answer these questions about you? Communication begins in the home first but there is a whole world out there teaching our youth! How alarming is that?

Who's talking to our youth? Communication devices like television, radios, CD players and computers are main staples in our homes. The days of watching TV in the living room with your parents are long forgotten these days, the old black and white set with the rabbit ears to bring in the reception of the entire three available channels on (VHF) and the few (UHF) channels are no more. If you didn't already know the three major commercial television networks in the U.S. are the National Broadcasting Company (NBC), the Columbia Broadcasting System (CBS), which both began as radio networks, and the American Broadcasting Company (ABC), which also began as a radio network in 1943 when it broke from NBC. In those days networks actually signed off after a day of broadcasting; isn't that something you would find in Mr. Peabody and Sherman's Wayback Machine? I mean today, how many young people know that, once upon a time at one o-clock in the morning, there was no TV to watch because there was no broadcast signal?

"It's now 11 o'clock. Do you know where your children are?" This question would come across the air reminding parents that they are parents and have a responsibility to care for their youth. It's almost as if the network executives knew what constituted respectable behavior then. What happened to that? Now networks gladly assault and insult our intelligence as well as our sense of integrity. Individuals responsible for such degenerate TV programming are promoted and applauded by their colleagues and surprisingly by the viewing public as well.

In 1931 experimental TV broadcasts begin from high atop the Empire State Building. In 1939 NBC begins to broadcast regular programming. In 1948 television ownership reaches one million. Now jumping ahead only 86 years we find that in 2017 every home has at least two sets. You can get 300 or more channels on your TV with programming ranging from XXX rated pornography to the cartoon network, which, in my own personal opinion, airs programming depicting witchcraft and doctrines of demons on many of their programs. Parents, we need to look at some of what our youth are watching. We cannot consider these programs innocuous simply because it's packaged in cartoon format. Our children are left without adult supervision in their rooms at night and the broadcasting never signs off.

Sidebar: We are such good parents that want our young to have every convenience so we make sure that they have a TV, IPod, CD player, video game set, computer, and a cell phone with Internet capability in their rooms to plug themselves into the mind of the world. (In case you didn't realize it, that was my attempt at sarcasm!)

The Trojan horse called television has rendered many individuals, both young and not so young, defenseless to the continual assaults on their sense of values and ethical decency. It appears that desensitization to the ongoing moral decay and declining value system is the goal. As parents, we must remain standard bearers or the entire civilization in which we live could crumble. But as for TV we ourselves as caregivers bring the TV Trojan horse through the gate. We leave it for the most part unattended, allowing any form of destruction to disembark to the impairment of our youth — and right under our own very noses! Music videos, disgusting talk shows and their equally distasteful hosts do much to dismantle decency and moral ascent. So-called reality shows and the subject matter of many of the sitcoms are very distasteful but are being force-fed to a disarmed generation of TV viewers, infiltrating our cornea passing through to the neocortex through the blood-brain barrier and into the heart, producing damaging spiritual results.

Home life situations reflect primary ways in which we communicate and learn about the world around us. We learn coping strategies and how to operate within the framework of relationships primarily from our home life setting. As these coping strategies are incorporated into our day-to-day life and we become more community oriented, subconsciously we view our surroundings through the lens filter of what we learn through early interaction with parents and siblings. School and neighborhood friendships and associations are thusly impacted as we mature. TV, news headlines and advertising schemes help foster and strengthen core beliefs generated in early childhood.

Many outside influences strengthen or weaken our ability as youth to send and/or receive messages clearly or accurately, leaving us with unclear indicators of who we are or how to navigate through the maze of adolescent life.

Creation vs. evolution, obvious murderers being acquitted while innocent people are convicted, same gender sexual inter-course is applauded, political corruption, business corruption, capitalistic greed openly on display while other economic systems and forms of government are summarily altogether vilified when obviously not everything about them is faulty or in error. Money, money, money, money makes the world go round. No wait, isn't it love that makes the world go round? Whatever! Is it war or is it peace today? Sell! Sell! Sell! If you don't have my product you're allowing life to pass you by! Remember the song that proclaimed *"Signs, signs everywhere signs blocking out the scenery breaking my mind?"* So much to choose from it's almost a blur. As we provide messages to our youth, do we clarify as much as stupefy, confound and confuse?

Person-To-Person Communication

During the course of our daily grind we meet many people, some of whom have positive outlooks and are moving forward in honorable ways. Conversely, many people that we meet during our daily comings and goings can be taxing or draining because of their negative energy; they just seem to be toxic! Fresh perspectives most often come from fresh people. If I could use a pretzel analogy I would say the sooner you eat the pretzel after baking it, the fresher and more palatable it is. However, the longer the pretzel sits in the open air the less original it becomes. I'm sure you would understand my meaning if this could be applied to people from young to not so young.

My current focus requires a clearer viewpoint, so I spoke with younger individuals who haven't experienced the world to great extent over many decades. I met a young man of the age of 23 in a local computer lab. He appeared to have a firm grasp on the realities that life presented in his personal experiences. He appeared to understand what it would take to make the most of the opportunities presented to him. He is presently attending the local university, studying to become a physician. He has an outgoing, very gregarious, personality, and is very easy to talk to. I asked if I could pose a few questions, and he consented. He told me that his mother, brother, and savior Jesus Christ are the forces that drive and motivate him. Interestingly, he said that his parents have an impact in his life! Hmmm! *"Positive people, affirmative influences excite me,"* he said. He went further to say that *"My family of origin is composed of African American and maybe some Dominican and my parents are divorced. They divorced when I was very young and I was raised primarily by my mother with strong influence from my father. I thought about many different fields of medicine to pursue but I feel that dermatology or physician's assistant would be preferable to me."*

I asked him about two different possibilities that a doctor might encounter with the world being in such turmoil as it is; his answers were very interesting. I assured him that there was no right or wrong answers to either of these situations, just food for thought. How we view our surroundings and the people that comprise our world was what mattered to me.

First, I asked him if there was a bombing or accident of some kind and he was on the scene when it happened, and there were two individuals lying in need of immediate medical care and in peril of meeting their imminent demise as the seconds ebbed away; one being a 16-year-old African American male, another a 68-year-old Caucasian female. As a physician, which would you attend first if you were free to choose?

Surprisingly he said in 2015, *"I would attend the Caucasian female first. My first inclination would be to attend the Caucasian first because there are too many instances of racisms or hindsight biases. We should converge or come together. In the 50s and 60s racism was a large overcast in our society and here we are about to embark on 2017 and we should not still be stuck there."* I found his perspective on this topic to be somewhat refreshing and unique as a 23-year-old African American male. As he gave this response I somewhat recoiled, not in disbelief or rebuke, but in a pleasant affirmation of his reply as sincere. I found his response to be other than what I had expected. I agree that we have far too much racial divide in the world today, giving rise to segregation, racism, nationalism, political party-ism, all the way to the religious jihadists, who for the sake of their particular ism, will kill not only you and me but themselves as well; and with pleasure I might add. (Note: This interview occurred in 2015, but now we are about to embark on 2018.)

While I am not sure how I would answer that question myself, we can understand much from this young man's viewpoint. He said that he would treat the person based on race and not severity of injury or likelihood of successful prognosis; that's sort of reverse racism, isn't it? But we can still discern from his response that everything is not as it seems on the surface. In other words, you can't judge a book by its cover. To look at this young man I would conjecture that he was as many other young persons of his group are viewed. His appearance was like most of his cohorts.

Many could have conceived in their mind that he's a thug or maybe he's a menace to society, or just discounted him without another thought. After all his pants hang low, his hair is long and braided into dreads too, for Pete's sake! He also wears two long chains out of his pockets that reach almost to his knees for crying out loud! This man looks like somebody that you might see standing on the corner clockin.' I would be far too presumptuous as many are if I overlooked him based on these simple visual indicators. I think it happens too often that we pass judgment based on such external things.

But how refreshing it was to sit and talk to him; to hear his perspectives on things; to observe his intelligence and self-respect. He is a very likable individual. I don't think I'll run up to every young person I see and say, *"Hey let's talk; lets share our inner most thoughts and insights."* I am however encouraged that there could be something great behind the rough exterior of the young brown-eyed baby doll's cruel stare, or possibly untapped genius powerfully circulating through the mind of what so many see as a hip-hop hoodlum. Were we so different with our tight-fitting elephant bellbottom pants, leaping fro and our black power fist's a pumping? What about our long hippie hair? What about our peace signs and love-in's and acid dropping endeavors? What did our parents and the older generations think of us then?

My follow-up questions to this young man was, if your 16-year-old daughter came home with a communicable disease, would you have an automatic prepackaged response that she had engaged in inappropriate sexual behavior or otherwise unhealthy contact with someone? Would you then begin to express disapproval of her circumstantially obvious misconduct?

He retorted sharply: *"I would want my daughter to be able to come to me with any situation"* he answered. *"It is my desire that any of my children would be able to share their hurts as well as their joys with me. I would not approach her in a demonstrative way but at the same time I don't think I would treat it as if it was all right either. A great deal of diplomacy would need to be employed in this case. I would understand remembering that I was once 16."* That was his answer. Now, if it were me and my 16-year-old daughter had contracted an STD, I don't think my first reaction would be as sure or as calm as his.

Would I go over the top? I don't know; I doubt it. I would need to be as instrumental as I could be in helping with a remedy, but I don't think *"Let's sit down and rap about feelings"* would be my position either. Granted, he has no children yet, but I respect his answer as real and the true expression of his current belief. I reserve the privilege of talking to him after he has had a few kids and shared his experiences, hopes and future dreams with them for 16 years; then I'll ask him that question once again and see how calmly he would react.

Nevertheless, let's envision a world in which we as parents talked to, instead of at, our children and our children really discussed their life issues with us. I'm talking about a world where time is set aside in our homes for genuine communication to take place. Wow! That sounds like a world apart from the world in which we presently live.

(Suddenly I can almost see Ward and the Beaver sitting at the dining room table talking over the Beav's latest foul up while June quietly bakes some muffins in the kitchen, wearing her pump high heels, a neat dress with coordinated beads around her neck. Gee what a swell scene!)

OK, reality check! I'm awake now; let's move on. I must have dozed off for a moment there. The reality is we spend very little time conversing in meaningful ways with our youth. We tell them what to do and what not to do. What road shall we pursue to alter this unprofitable method of sharing or the lack thereof with our youth?

Another young person that I have had the pleasure of knowing from the time she was a baby is my niece, Adrienne. She is now a college student and has declared that she intends to enter medical school also. Adrienne is preparing her thesis and I was thrilled at hearing her declaration because she has always impressed me as an intelligent, hardworking, and very pleasant person from whom I have always expected great things. I have never altered that perception I've held of her. I asked her about her motivation to become a doctor and here is what she stated:

"I am now 19 years old and will be 20 on May 15th. The reason I decided to go into the medical field was because I knew that I wanted to help people. I have always tried to play doctor. When I was little I would find little abandoned rabbits, kittens, and birds and try to take care of them. The reason that I want to become a pediatrician is because I love kids, and would like to help them get better.

"The thing that motivates me most is... my brother, who died of cancer at the age of 3 and becoming a pediatrician would help me to help other kids just like him.

"His passing also shaped me into the person that I am today. I consider myself to be a nice person. I believe the reason for that is, I understand how valuable and precious life is. My life is blessed; the world is colorful and I would like my lasting legacy to be that hopefully I may help find a cure for cancer.

"God is very important in young people's lives including my own. I need God for everything and pray to Him for everything. I ask for Him to guide me in the direction that I am meant to go,

and ask Him to make me the person He wants me to be and He has really been leading me that way. I just have to follow. All my accomplishments are because of Him. He makes everything possible in my life. Sometimes the road gets tough but those bumps are there for a reason and it strengthens me and makes me into the person I am today.

"When I was in high school I was selected to be on the homecoming court my sophomore, junior, and senior years. I think that I was chosen because I am nice to people. I am the type of person that sees the good in everyone and I try my hardest not to gossip. I am very easy to get along with, and I participated in a lot of clubs and activities so I knew a lot of people.

"I think that the over 40 generation can do much in order to make the world a better place for today's youth and their offspring. That generation should teach the youth, love them, and to be there for them. There are so many young people that I know that do not have a father around and they are bitter and angry at the world, causing them to do things that may not be in their character. They are really good people when you get know them."

Adrienne tapped into the heart of what I am attempting to convey in this book with her comment about one generation teaching, loving, and being there for future generations. Adrienne has a very positive outlook on life, and by contrast to some of the negativity that is so pervasive in present day culture, she has not allowed it to paint her world.

Much of the irritation with establishment politics and positions felt by youth I believe comes from the fact that we of the baby boom generation have become callous and indifferent to the concerns of youth. This is a mindset that filters our relations with many youths. We are still attempting to make it big, better, and best for ourselves. Along the way however, it seems that the economy has shifted and the types of economic upsurge that we began with in the 1950s and 1960s is no longer as vibrant as it once was, and we are still in search of it as one who has lost his own shadow. Turning in circles, we search for what has become very elusive for the vast majority of people.

There is a film titled *Over the Edge*, produced by George Litto. It is touted as a real story of teenage rebellion. This story, written by Charlie Haas, shows a community absorbed in suburban life concerns and its trappings. This community has affluent and not so well to do families whose youth are in the mix together. It's about tomorrow's city today; a planned suburban paradise. But something has been left out of the plans; no one is paying attention to the town's teens. It's about kids left to discover their own values and having enough money to buy all the drugs and booze they want. What the teens really want is their parents love and consideration. But what they get is dissatisfaction, which is enough to push everyone over the edge.

This film was actually filmed about ten miles from where the Columbine school tragedy took place. I would suggest that everyone reading this book view the film also; it dramatizes much of what is being outlined here. In the film, the teens rebel in an unforgettable firestorm of violent vengeance. Let us ask ourselves, are we in some way frustrating today's youth, similarly as that which is depicted in the movie? Are we seeing mass rebellion similar to that seen in the film *Over the Edge*?

One's life can be summed up as a total of experiences and how we learn from them. Do we teach our youth caring, and love for his and her fellows? Is our conduct honorable enough to garner their respect and admiration? What do we communicate to our youth? We live and learn as we go. If we are wise we understand that each one has something to teach us. Not all lessons are meant to provide us with paths to follow. Some lessons are meant to show us the roads to avoid. I ask myself often, which lesson my life demonstrates? How about you? Selah! That is, pause and reflect on these words!

(I added interviews in this book because I did indeed learn much from other individuals and the experiences they communicated. What I have learned I am attempting to pass on to others.)

There is another individual whom I have had the pleasure of knowing since my years in grade school. Knowing him and watching his life develop over many years of friendship provided some insights for me as well. We share many of the same interests, played sports together, and graduated high school in the same class. As we began to come into adolescence we did what many boys do at that stage of life, meaning that we talked about girls; the ones we liked and the ones nobody seemed to like. We made jokes about some of our cohorts; we went to music concerts and experimented with alcohol and marijuana. We studied for exams, played sports and just laughed a lot.

I can recall one very memorable incident that was not very much fun to me personally. He and I, along with two other boys who were friends of ours, were standing along the side of the street. We were sharing a beer and smoking some pot when a woman came down that street driving very erratically and she almost ran us down. She was shouting out of the window that the rapture had taken place and we were all left behind. Needless to say, I was very disturbed to say the least. As a child, my mother regularly took us to church for as far back as I can remember. I knew what this lady was talking about when she said that the Lord had already come and we were left behind. I had heard many sermons regarding the rapture. I do however believe sometimes some preachers try to frighten you into becoming more loyal to them or their congregations by painting horrific images of a post-rapture Earth with colorful sermons and antichrist inferences. According to scriptures, nonetheless these things will happen...and I sure want to be on the Lord's side now as well as when these apocalyptic events finally do take place.

Notwithstanding, if it was due to the pot and drink, I believed that what this lady was talking about was real and happening right then. When this lady came nearby us shouting about this very foreboding subject matter I could not be consoled because it was very real to me. I got on my bike and hustled to the church that we attended because I was sure that this was a lady from our particular congregation.

Moreover, my mother, who was a very devout Christian woman, was at church Bible study this particular evening. I felt that if the rapture had come, certainly she would be taken. But if I could set my eyes on her I might feel that maybe I was mistaken and this lady was just loony or maybe I had smoked too much pot. After peddling as fast as my youthful legs could peddle I got to the church and much to my dismay no one was there. My heart raced even faster, now it was on to plan B. If I could call home and my mother was there then maybe, just maybe, I could be relieved of my desperation.

Back on my bike I once again peddled like 90 going north in hyper drive. I may be dating myself somewhat but pay phones were almost everywhere at that time and only 10 cents per call. Wow, how retro! Cell phones were still something that you only saw on *Star Trek*. Anyway, I traveled to the nearest pay phone and put in my dime to place my call. Nervously I dialed the number: one ring, two rings, then three; my dad rarely answered the phone so my expectation was that if he answered it means mom is not home and if she isn't home then — Wheeerrreee isss sheee?

Well on about the fifth ring the receiver was picked up; it was as if it took 35 minutes for someone to say *"Hello."* To my relief it was mom. What a reprieve. My friends who were there that day never let me off the hook for that. They really gave me the horse laugh but imagine the horror I experienced in that moment. Real or imagined, it was true to me at that point in time.

I shared many adventures and countless hours with my good friend doing what makes youthful exuberance what it is. Mind you, all youth do not select the path that we experimented with, but as a point of contrast and seeing how our lives veered in different directions from there, I have asked myself many times, what made the difference? Why was he able to climb to such lofty heights while for so long I lingered in those lowly pursuits?

After we grew up and entered adulthood my friend and I married our sweethearts. I got married first and shortly after-wards he married a very nice girl that we went to school with.

You know how life tracks you in different directions some-times and you lose sight of old friends? In this case I have been fortunate enough to be able to keep in touch with him as the years rolled by. He has two children, a son and a daughter. They are both college graduates and his son is preparing to use his degree in the U.S. Air Force. I am very impressed with him and his wife in regard to how they raised their children with such good values. Allan and Balinda were able to provide their children with such proper guidance that they both appear to have positive present and future trajectories.

Their daughter is an equestrian who has won several prestigious awards for her riding. He and his wife are employed by the university and their marriage is a strong union which has lasted for over 30 years. There is a lot that I could say about what makes some youths track well and others not so well, but it would be mostly speculative at best.

In my opinion, strong family ties with values that are constantly upheld and reinforced through demonstration have a great deal of impact on how one will develop. Communication, love, and understanding are also invaluable components to raising emotionally healthy youth. What could have caused me and my close friend to offshoot into the contrasting directions that we took when we were so closely linked as teens? While we remain close friends today our lives and the lives of our children are very dissimilar. He was not as invested in this experimentation with the lifestyle of diversion while I lingered there for many more years to the ruin of many of my life opportunities. My children saw my shame. I can offer some possibilities for the evolving divergence in our lives and our children's lives based on my personal experience and careful study vs. his childhood and the upbringing he experienced.

Communication with parents, grandparents and so forth down the line are key elements to successful self-images. We all have a choice in how we live our lives. I blame no one for the choices that I knowingly made. I often wonder why I selected the less quality option. And he was able to select a less cluttered pathway. He has unbroken communication with both his parents. I believe he is able to talk openly with his parents about any circumstance or possibility that may occur in his life. And his parents share their hurts, failures, and triumphs with him as well.

Some families, such as mine, have secrets or certain things that cannot be discussed with parents or laterally with siblings; things that are taboo. We just didn't talk about the real issues. I have heard the saying that we are as sick as our secrets. Families, individuals, communities, and large groups of peoples have unspoken traumas. Trauma to specific areas of the body causes bruising or other linked injury. If there is a huge dinosaur in the middle of the living room, he must be acknowledged and dealt with; if not, his ravenous appetite will devour those living in the house. His elimination deposits will bring a stench and ultimately disease. It's necessary to communicate the evidence of such apparitions in our midst. Everyone already knows it's there and when we push it under the rug we do a disservice to all involved.

Emotional bruising and mental trauma can have effects that last a lifetime. Secrets held from others are tough, but probably most damaging are the secrets we hold deep below the surface away from our own cognitive recognition; these do much harm to our emotional well-being. Disclosure and communication provide opportunities to work things out and foster greater understanding. It is difficult for me even to write that there were such secrets in my family of origin; hurtful secrets. Youthful minds and emotions translate experiences into core belief systems about themselves and the world around them. What we demonstrate in the presence of our youth will communicate impressions to them of who they are and of what their world consists.

"Call the Cops!" Momma shrieked with terror in her voice! As all five of us kids huddled together, eyes fixed on daddy and ma on the floor furiously fighting. We moved cautiously toward the phone at momma's behest. *"Don't you call nobody,"* daddy said. In his voice, there was an assurance that if we did, we would get the same rude treatment momma was getting on that dusty kitchen floor.

Still huddled together, we moved away from the phone at the command of daddy's angry voice. *"Call em,"* momma exclaimed, now moving back closer to the phone as one befuddled unit, we went to make the call. *"I said you better not call anybody,"* daddy yelled! Sluggishly the group of us five children moved together away from the phone, unsure of what to do.

A hard right then a left, oh' a smashing uppercut! Now the strangle hold, eyes bulging, gasping for air, arms and legs flailing. The World Wrestling Entertainment, Inc. couldn't create an improved upon fight if they had Hulk Hogan coming off of the top rope with an elbow smash to "Macho Man" Randy Savage's throat, causing him to vomit blood onto front row spectators. But this was real, not some choreographed dance made up by Vince McMahon. This was real life; this was our life; this was our secret.

Then the cast iron skillet appeared as if from nowhere. Momma reared back with it and came down hard. Blood rained all over the kitchen floor. Completely traumatized we stood there in a huddled mass of youthful horror as we witnessed the nightmarish occurrence. We cried vehemently because it was all we could do. Somehow momma got out to the car and attempted to start it up and leave. However, true to every horror picture you've ever seen of course, the car wouldn't start until daddy got out there. Daddy ran out and got in on the passenger side still bleeding profusely from the gash on his hand. The skillet had broken into pieces when mom hit him with it, leaving blood and shards of cast iron all over the floor. Then the fight started all over again in the front seat of the car, located in the garage.

"Auntie, is daddy beaten up Momma out there?" My aunt who lived a couple doors away had come over due to all the commotion. *"Looks more like she is getting the better of him,"* came back the answer. Can't much remember what happened the next day but one thing I do remember, this imagery replayed itself over and over and over again as down through the years arguing fussing and fighting became the culture in which we lived. *"You betanot tell nobody"* was the motto that drove this hurt deeper into my emotional recesses as the tempo of the years gained momentum steadily moving forward, steadily compounding more weight and deeper dimensions.

Truth is, I am still encumbered with the weight of those images. The puppy dog size rats that scurried through the bedrooms as I tried to sleep added a frightening layer of icing on that dreadful cake of disbelief. "Whap" went the sound of the traps under the kitchen sink as we sat eating breakfast before school. The monstrous rodent struggling to free himself made such eerie reverberations that they still echo in the inner workings of my soul. The thrashing about became less and less as the strangle hold of the trap took its toll. Us kids sitting at the table eating breakfast looked at each other but said nothing. We learned to repress at an early age.

All of our parent's friends and relations repeatedly would declare, *"My' they are doing such a good job with raising those kids, oh my! See how well behaved they are,"* they would say, as I stood there traumatized by what goes on when the door has been shut. Soon all would-be onlookers and witnesses to these nightmarish recurrences would be once again outside the gate, unaware of what goes on behind closed doors.

Anguish doesn't have to be obvious to everyone else. Some things reside within the inner dimensions of one's soul, unseen by the outside world, but the images replay like a broken record on the heart of the individual's hard drive. They replay over and over until it becomes a part of you, just like your nose or your hands. What would you feel if the person who you saw deliver such brutal punishment over the years told you that he felt that he should cut off your head simply because you had a headache? Someone who you idolized and believed would not lie to you! My own father told me that more than once. Would you feel frightened and confused? Well, that's what I felt! Once again, Selah! Pause and reflect on these words!

My parents are very good people, please do not misinterpret what I am saying. What I am attempting to communicate is that they simply operated on the foundational principals which they possessed at that time. In turn, all I could function by was what I saw and heard or learned. My children likewise will grow up to emulate the same practices that pass from one generation to the next unless at some point these practices are interrupted. Not surprisingly my father witnessed similar flaws in his parent's relationship. We must not only interrupt unfruitful traditions but we must replace them with more beneficial methods.

My children have seen some of the same "less than romantic" images displayed before them as their mother and I wrestled to seize dominance in our household. These are the same images that she and I both witnessed as youths growing up in our separate homes with our parents. And not surprisingly my children have had similar struggles in their relationships. How far back does this relationship model go in our family's history? And when will we cut the ties to this unprofitable practice and begin demonstrating understanding, begin giving and receiving love and affection with our most solid companion in the spirit of tenderness and gentle humility? This type of generational communication that passes from parent to child and to grandchild will not come to an end by itself. We must recognize it and purposefully banish it from our family trees. Our descendants will not have to combat the same wars that we can win today. So, let's win it now!

"So much of what we know of love we learn at home." — Author unknown

There is a saying taken from the pages of the owner's Manual which pronounces that we are to love the Lord with all our ability and our neighbor as ourselves. Many families have lost the ability to show each other love. It doesn't mean that love is not there, it simply becomes difficult to demonstrate it somehow, or one's model of love could be tainted. Sometimes after harsh words or trying times spent in close quarters with the individuals we spend most of our daily lives with, the warmth of love chills. Truly loving couples end in divorce for this very reason. We become so common with each other and carelessly say and do things without love and compassion. We become more self-driven, attempting to meet our selfish wants and needs without regard to the one we truly do love. The end product is that we become sightless of the needs of our loved ones.

My friend's father will kiss him, and tell him he loves him, and he is free to reciprocate as he desires to express it. I have witnessed this with my own eyes. On the other hand, with my parents, to date, I cannot remember more than one or two times hearing them express verbally or affectionately to one another that they love each other. I however know that in a perplexing way they do love one another. It's hard to explain!

I do not remember them expressing love in any affectionate way to me either, although they made sure that I had everything tangibly that I needed. Affection and open display of love and compassion were vividly absent in our home. I remember seeing mom and dad kiss one Christmas; it seemed rather odd!

I believe that the spiritual world is more authentic than the world we can see with our natural eyes. What we cannot see with our physical eyes can be discerned in a more reliable way than that which is handled or touched with the sense of touch, taste, smell, sight, or hearing. Love being the greatest of these things. As parents, as mom and dad, we must make absolutely sure that our youth know that we love each other and love them as well. I believe that a primary reason we possess the ability to communicate is so we can share the emotion of love with family, friends, and neighbors.

Maslow's "Hierarchy of needs" has "belongings" and "love" as needs number three, eclipsed in ranking of importance only by physiological and safety needs. Once we know that our heart is beating, we are still breathing and have food and safe shelter, and if possible decent covering, we then move to the next level, the level of belongingness and love

This third layer of human need is negotiated socially. This psychological aspect of Maslow's hierarchy involves emotionally based relationships in general, such as having friends and intimacy. Having a supportive and communicative family structure is listed as very important. If we understand primate and whale families we see this same dynamic at work. Humans need to feel a sense of belongingness, love and acceptance. Whether it comes from a large social group like church, neighborhood group, or work, is not the most central factor the fact that this need is met is the key. Organizations such as sports teams and even gangs provide the necessary fulfillment of this particular need if it is not met in a more primary way, such as in a traditional family. There must be a love component to people's lives. Loving and being loved (sexually and/or non-sexually) is indispensable to one's total well-being.

"Love is a fruit in season at all times, and within reach of every hand." — Mother Teresa

The Manual speaks clearly about love in this way, as I para-phrase: Love is unwearied and love is sympathetic. It does not envy, it does not brag, it is not arrogant or rude, it is not self-seeking, it is not easily angered, it keeps no record of wrongs. Love does not delight in evil but rejoices with the truth. It always covers, always trusts, always hopes, and always perseveres. Love is never unsuccessful. But where there are prophecies, they will cease; where there are tongues, they will be stilled; where there is knowledge, it will pass away. For we know in part and we prophesy in part, but when perfection comes, the imperfect disappears. When I was a child, I talked like a child; I thought like a child, I reasoned like a child. When I became a man, I put childish ways behind me. Now we see but a poor reflection as in a mirror; then we shall see face-to-face. Now I know in part, then I shall know fully, even as I am fully known. And now these three remain: faith, hope and love. But the greatest of these is love.

Communicating this thing called love to those near us is of the upmost significance as it relates to real growth and develop-ment. It is as if we were structured into community living for the purpose of sharing God with each other through love. For God is love. Our testimony of Him to the next generation is communicated through our love. In the absence of love what have we truly given?

We can deduct from (The most purchased book in history) the Bible's inference of the importance of love and how it emphasizes just how much God loves us through the great love of Christ. Additionally, from Maslow's hierarchical theory we learn that knowing, experiencing, and feeling love are indispensable components to healthy human existence. Love is not a tangible substance like gold or food, but love is a more existent commodity to the true self than gold or food; God is love! We must receive and then communicate love to our offspring and they must in turn forward it to their progeny. Love is a currency that must be spent in order that it may flow back to us. I believe that my friend and his wife love each other very much and their kids know it. It does something portentous to kids when mom and dad refuse to love each other, or come apart in some form of separation, or otherwise demonstrate constant hostility toward each other.

Conversely, when the unbroken bond of fellowship is known and understood with love and compassion being there for the family unit, youth can blossom. Familiarity with love and communicating love provides youths in such home settings with a nurturing atmosphere in which they can flourish and enlarge their platform for greater success. My friend's kids know that they are loved by their parents also. The children love and respect their parents in kind, doing well for themselves and I believe they do well as a means of giving pleasure to mom and dad also. My wife and I ended our relationship in divorce. Perhaps because of this separation, our children have not become as successful relationally as they may have otherwise been. The communication of love between their mother and I broke down as our relationship as husband and wife deteriorated. Although I love our children very much, it's as if a disconnection from the power source happened and somehow the love message to my kids has been stymied. I believe that communication is best utilized when it is primarily the conveyance mechanism of God's currency: love. Youth experience life by the same human spirit as we adults do; we cannot hide the truth from them. When we fail they know it; when we succeed they know it. It is therefore incumbent upon us to know what true success or failure is.

"Woe to the man whose heart has not learned while young to hope, to love — and to put its trust in life." — Joseph Conrad

Chapter Three

The Youth Crime Paradigm

John Hoover, otherwise known as J. Edgar Hoover (January 1, 1895 – May 2, 1972), was the first Director of the Federal Bureau of Investigation, or FBI. Mr. Hoover was instrumental in founding the FBI in 1935, where he remained the Director until his death in 1972. Mr. Hoover is attributed with building the FBI into the large and efficient crime-fighting agency we know it to be today. He instituted a number of modern innovations to police technology while seated as Director of the FBI.

In 1936 Mr. Hoover gave a speech[1] at the Chicago Boys Club wherein he stated that, "*The American home is our foremost battlefront*" in the fight against crime. He noted that when parents search for the reason why their child chose a life of crime, many must simply, *"look in the mirror"* to find the answer to that question. A husband and wife must ask themselves, *"Where did we fail?"* According to Mr. Hoover, they failed to teach their children to respect the property of others, and therefore failed to prevent their children from taking possessions which do not belong to them.

Mr. Hoover also correctly stated that, "*The father who envies the lifestyle of the gangsters and the big wad of cash they have stuffed into their pockets,*" and displays such envious behavior in front of his children, is *"wittingly or unwittingly painting a picture of romance."* The father also paints a romanticized picture of crime when, in front of his children, he talks about the financial advantages of gambling or gloats when criminals successfully evade the police. Simply stated, he is teaching his children that crime does pay, and that the life of a *"super-gangster"* may be more rewarding and exciting than the life of a moral, law-abiding citizen.

Mr. Hoover further talked about the role of the mother as well when he said, *"The fatuous mother who would rather play bridge intemperately than stand guard over the morals or the associates of her daughter has no excuse whatever when that daughter, without guidance, without protection or parental advice strays into the cheap dance hall or the roadside tavern, sneaks into the cocktail bar, runs with other girls and men with low moral character and herself finally takes an existence as the paramour of a crook."* According to Mr. Hoover, through such negligence, a mother becomes an accomplice to the crimes of her daughter, whether she did so *"wittingly or unwittingly."*

Because of the crucial role parent's play in raising their children to either respect the law or embrace a life of crime, crime prevention must include education of the parents as well as the education of their children: *"They must be made to realize that a home is, after all, a cradle of endeavor. It can be good endeavor or it can be bad endeavor, as the parents care to make it. And we who can think clearly must view the picture of disaster which faces us and consecrate ourselves to the crusade of education, not only for the children but also for the parents."*

The words of Mr. Hoover's speech are just as relevant today as they were in 1936. Parents are in places of great influence in families and can be guideposts for good or for evil as it relates to the children in their home.

Participation in crime and below standard behaviors are facets of performance demonstrated by acceptance-hungry individuals converging from a wide range of backgrounds and socio-economic circumstances.

Stark County's Treatment Accountability for Safer Communities Agency, or TASC, is a private, non-profit organization within the heart of Ohio where a case manager, Mr. Kevin Goode, provided me with the following information regarding youth in

Middle and Northeast Ohio. His efforts to assist youth in channeling their energies away from negative pursuits and toward pursuits which are more beneficial to themselves and the community are well noted.

He said, "*The youths within my caseload ranged from ages 13 through 20 and the crimes committed vary from stealing to murder. Although most of my cases involve males I have an almost equal number of females.*"

He went on to say "*The youths I deal with are in my opinion good kids but simply became involved with the wrong crowd due to peer pressure. There is a high rate of sexual activity and STD's that typify the lives of these youth*" he said. "*Unwanted pregnancies are also prevalent. It appears that the individuals who are creating the pregnancies and passing the STD's involve many of the same youths who commit the crimes. They apparently are acquainted with each other sexually as well as in the participation of various crimes.*"

Interestingly enough, he surmises that "*Roughly 20 percent of my cases involve youths who live in single parent homes and of that number there is a high occurrence of situations where youth are living with brothers and sisters with little or no parental involvement. Many show signs of aggression or forwardness which they do not recognize as such but simply see their behavior as culturally acceptable or customary.*" He related to me that "*It appears that entitlement issues have surfaced with the belief that the world owes something that was not conveyed earlier on. Possibly as a result of clever advertising schemes individuals may feel that they aren't successful because they don't have all the up-to-date items. Many youths may feel somehow deprived if they do not have the modern things.*

"*While many crimes committed in society today involve drug activity where subsequent corrections become necessary; it doesn't appear that drug activity is the overarching theme here"* he said. *"It appears that other issues have fostered an atmosphere where involvement in inappropriate behavior has become the norm for the individuals in most of these specific circumstances,"* he said.

In order to gain wider perspective on the topic of youth and crime I also spoke with Detective Donnie Whitworth, Police Community Relations D.A.R.E Officer with the Akron Police Department. Detective Whitworth shared with me that he has been with the police department for 38 years and during that time span has observed no real or appreciative changes in community activity. He began his work with youth as a D.A.R.E. Officer in 1992 because he enjoys assisting young individuals and teaching them about the dangers of drug use and the consequences of violence. Officer Whitworth stated that:

"The knowledge I provide youth with aids them in their effort to make decisions that will help them take positive advantage of their lives."

The D.A.R.E. program targets youth ranging from grade level five through middle school.

"In my personal opinion D.A.R.E. has had a positive impact in the lives of youths who participated in it; students who I taught as very young children have progressed to become lawyers and other professionals, some of whom have come to me and shared that they remember the things I told them. They say that it was beneficial in their overall success as a person. The young people I am referring to also came from good families so I'm not sure if it was the family values or the impact I had with the D.A.R.E. program, probably a bit of both," officer Whitworth said.

What Officer Whitworth said in regard to family values also echo's what Mr. Hoover stated to the youths in his Chicago speech. D.A.R.E. is the international trademark for the *Drug-Abuse-Resistance-Education* program, in partnership with police officers, parents and schools. Detective Whitworth went on to share with me that the program is national in its scope and began in Los Angeles in the 80s. *"Youth crime is on the rise because respect for authority is absent and there is no fear of consequence anymore,"* he admitted.

He further stated that gang violence is on the rise also, and much to my surprise he reported that Ohio is fourth in the nation in gang activity after California, Texas and Illinois. According to the Detective, *"Lack of traditional family standards may be one primary reason for the upsurge in gang and violent activity."* He further described how violence and gang activities are visually supported by gangster or hip-hop lifestyles as seen in videos, movies and on TV programs. *"Biggie Smalls and Tupac Shakur and the lifestyles they portrayed have had tremendous impact on the life of today's youth"* the Detective said. *"Instead of looking at Willie Mays or Michael Jordan the gangster figures are idolized; Medgar Evers fought for equality in the 50s and 60s, now people take what they want with a gun or sling dope.*

"Back in the day we related to the Cosby Show and before that we watched Julia with Diane Carol, but somehow Cosby became not black enough and I don't know what the networks are doing but the shows now are more urban and racy," he said.

Detective Whitworth has been a fine addition to the Akron police force for the 38 years he has served. During our interview, we sat comfortably in the office of the Community Relations Department.

As our conversation proceeded he would periodically take phone calls from community residents to answer various questions. Detective Whitworth also was busy giving direction to office staff between his answers to my questions. Officers would also pass through in the course of their duties as we sat there talking. With Whitworth's calm, easygoing demeanor, he made it relaxing for me to be there in the police station, otherwise being in a police station has an uneasy feeling for most, but I was made to feel at home.

My overall impression of what he was telling me about his experience with youth and crime is that it has been on the rise for a number of years and that ascent has not abated during his 38 year tenure. I understood him as saying that no real or appreciative change in the upward climb of certain crime statistics has occurred and it continues today as a result of new and more aggressive criminal methods and that we have been headed down this path toward ruin for a great while.

Family Ties

Here are just a few statistics that will help us understand the huge impact an intact, two-parent family has upon the development of the child when compared to the single-parent family:

According to a report titled *U.S. Single Parent Households,*[2] from 1980 to 2008, the number of single-parent households more than doubled. Using U.S. Census Bureau data, they further reported that, in 1980, 18.4% of all births in America were to unwed mothers. In 2008 the percent rose to 40.6%. This is a serious problem because *"70% of gang members, high school dropouts, teen suicides, teen pregnancies and teen substance abusers come from single mother homes."* Employing data from the *Single Parent Success Foundation,*[3] they reported that 63% of suicides nationwide, 75% of children in chemical dependency hospitals, and more than 50% of all youths incarcerated in the U.S. lived in one-parent families as a child.

I think much of the inequity between mothers and fathers having the children in their homes as a single parent is in large part due to the gender biases and unfairness of domestic courts and the child support industry which seem to have parallel conception stories sort of like creation vs. evolution.

One story is that the children are suffering and the state must do something to help the poor deserving children. While the concept of saving the children is valiant and may have had plausibility at the inception of the program, it has undoubtedly evolved into a more lucrative untold state by state business enterprise. The untold story is that this industry is in place to produce jobs and to generate income and a tax base for economically famished states.

Additionally, the child support revolution keeps men involved in an economic system that self-perpetuates because we cannot seem to stop committing fornication, divorce and adultery. States and counties capitalize on our lack of moral integrity. Additionally, the divorce rates are sky-high, leaving kids in the in-betweens. These same state governing bodies having power to levy punitive measures which ensnares with a wide net those individuals who are not closely socialized into this lynch mob mentality system. By becoming socialized into the system, I mean bringing in a whopping sum of money each month to keep the wheels of this machine greased and turning smoothly. If you are a slow pay or no pay dad, you're labeled deadbeat and ultimately deeper into the system you go. Resulting in Mo money, Mo money, Mo money, and Mo money for the states or counties and the individual falls right into the net. If you do pay in a timely manner, it's still more money for the states or counties. Men wise up! Everybody gets paid but you, so dig deep and find either some integrity or some cash, like the commercial says, *"What's in your wallet?"*

According to *America's Families and Living Arrangements: 2011*,[4] published by the United States Census Bureau, never-married parent homes are becoming more common as part of the single-parent home picture. For example, the number of unmarried parents living with their children in 2011 was 13.6 million. Of these, 10.0 million were unmarried mothers and 1.7 million were unmarried fathers, and 1.9 million were unmarried couples with at least one shared child.

Although there may be no direct, causal link between single-parent families, youth crime and violence, poor parenting is often identified as one of the most serious risk factors that prevent healthy youth development. The pressure of one individual performing the tasks that traditionally had been performed by two can be taxing in many ways which can result in the unintended consequence of shortchanging the child.

I had the pleasure of sitting down with a single mom who shared some of her opinions and personal history with me regarding single motherhood. She is a person who I believe to be a good mother and an accomplished person of the highest quality. *"My child is an 11-year-old male"* she told me. *"He attends public school and his grades are OK. My parents were never married and I have two brothers and one sister."* Once again we see a generational link between the way parents and their youth identify how to structure lifestyles with her being a never-married mother and her parents never being married. *"My father passed away a few years ago"* she shared. *"I think today's youth needs guidance from parents as well as teachers, boys and girls clubs, and other community entities. It is also very important in my personal opinion that two-parent homes are provided for today's youth. One reason among others is that the financial challenges of a mother alone can become great. On a scale of one to 10 the importance of the awareness of God and structure in a youth's life ranks at a 10 in my book"* she said. *"It is also very important for boys to have strong father figures because there are some things that a mother cannot teach her son. As a single mother, my hope for my child is realized on an everyday progressive basis, when I see my child doing better than I myself have done. From day one my desire has been for my child to be better, have better, and grow stronger than that which I have or could have experienced."*

We hear far too much about deterioration of the family nowadays. Stories seem to be negative ones about violence and parent's failures to properly care for their young or the aged members of the family and we hear so much of, where have the "good old days" gone? (Federal statistics show rising divorce rates, how three in 10 births are illegitimate, or the disappear-ance of the Ward and June Cleaver family model)

Perhaps family models are prototypes for all other social relations and the family unit is simply and accurately stated a fundamental building block in all societies. Family is society's shock-absorber of social change. We sit at home with our families and attempt to help each other make sense out of what's going on in the world. We love, have compassion and sympathy for one another as well as support each other by encouraging our family members when they try new and challenging things.

When our family member plays on the sports team we attend and cheer them on. When a family member is ill and in the hospital, we rally around them with get well wishes. When one of our family members gets married we travel great distances to be there in support of them. And when a member of our family dies, no matter what feelings or perceptions we may have held of them during their lifetime, we gather in celebration of their life and recall the impact that they had on us. When one member is in a fight, the rest of the family fights in defense of the family honor.

When I was a young boy the Key family was large. I believe about 10 strong; I think six boys and four girls. It was well known that if you get into it with any one of them, you had to fight them all. I guess it's true that there is safety in numbers. One cannot expect a person to do more for a stranger or an acquaintance than what he or she would do for a family member. However, increasingly we see family that will not communicate or have much to do with certain members of their own family unit.

There are many friends or other acquaintances that take precedence over a brother or a sister in some families, and surprisingly many times friends take precedence over our very own children. Family is community, together they are like Humpty Dumpty sitting on the wall and if he falls, and is broken, *"neither all the king's horses nor all the king's men will be able to put 'society' back together again,"* because family is the glue that binds us together in the larger societal composition.

Family however appears to be weakening in strength and veracity these days. Like peddling a bicycle up a long steep incline, one gets tired and begins to labor just to maintain forward motion; so it appears to be with the traditional family. The pure uncontaminated family is an essential part of our society that is progressively morphing into something different in many instances from what it was just 40 fleeting years ago. The family unit must be maintained as the fundamental societal building block that it has been for hundreds or thousands of years. Each of us must take a hard look at where the family is headed and make diligent efforts to ensure family stability. If the family is unstable our societies will be unstable as well. Unstable societies give rise to crime and all nature of criminal mischief and troublemaking behaviors.

Another facet of single parenting which can stymie personal growth and produce less than proper emotions and lead to uncommon behavior is also emotional in nature. Single mother-hood may be a necessary function in this postmodern society but sometimes mother/son relations become blurred or misunder-stood by those involved. Sometimes it appears that sons get confused as to what the difference is between son-ship and husband. And sadly, mothers many times find it difficult to make that total distinction as well. With the advent of unchecked fornication, adultery and divorce, many women find themselves raising children by themselves. Oftentimes after long periods of mother and son living as a unit unto themselves, when attempts are made to reintroduce another man into the home, the relationship is met at the door with resistance and confrontation by the young sons. After a young son is either told that he is the man of the house or simply assumes that role due to its vacancy, I have found that things may tend to get kind of weird in some cases.

I have witnessed single mothers and their sons maintaining relationships that are very potent and passionate, the relation-ships at times taking on the aura of husband and wife in a peculiar way. Of course, not all mother/son relations are so situated but this appears more common than one may think. At times I believe that the complicated relations between the two muddies or blurs the appropriate or more fitting connections and unfitting ties may develop.

I have observed nearly 20-year-old young men still sleeping in bed with their mother. I have also witnessed mothers who find it difficult to distinguish between proper affection toward her second or third husband or boyfriend and her sons. In addition, the son's rivalry with the new man in mom's life is a topic that need not be discussed here. I'm sure we all know about how so many second and third marriages crumble because of stress placed on them due to the son's refusal to allow mom to love another man. The sons in these cases demand her love and affection for themselves alone, and mom seemingly feeling that somehow, she is betraying sacred trusts if she loves her second or third husband completely.

It appears that mothers who find themselves in these bizarre triangles find it difficult to love a man as the man in her life and not provide her son with the same manner of emotional bond and in some cases affection.

Also, fathers developing incestuous relations with step-daughters, and even viler, violating their own flesh and blood daughters, are creating painful family life for the child and family stress for all involved.

How many times do we hear about school teachers and his or her student's being caught having sexual affairs? The harm done to the minds and emotions of our youth by such unconscionable acts committed by adults entrusted with their care in many cases are irrevocable. At best, it takes the youth well into adulthood to work through the dense jungle of twisted emotions and psychological damaged which has been left in the aftermath of the carelessness of such perpetrators.

Undoubtedly the overwhelming majority of youths never experience such traumatic episodes but probably all know at least one or more of their cohorts that have.

The balance of genuineness caused by what is happening anywhere impacts what is happening everywhere. The camaraderie between cohorts, whether it is the single mothers group, or the son and his friends, or the father who violated his daughter and his cohorts, or the daughter and her friends, they seem to find ways to validate each other. Mothers who say things like, *"My son will take care of that,"* or *"He is quite the man around the house."* Or the son when talking to other sons of unwed mothers may say things like, *"That so-and-so better not touch my mom or else."*

Emotions are fragile and it's difficult to be sure that the positives outweigh the negatives in such perplexing relations. For some puzzling rationale, it appears that we humans are more prone to allowing negatives to impose more force to the undoing of positives than the positive forces have on repelling negatives. This gives rise to a descending lifestyle pattern of sorts.

As generations progress from one to the next, more structured and widespread dimensions of moral degeneration continues to emerge. As neighborhoods and communities are formed along with the concrete structures of our houses, buildings and roads, we also develop social constructs. Constructs of immorality, decadence, collapse and ruin, which are built right into the fabric of our societies and passed on to our youth to build upon for future generations. Crime, misdeeds and hostility, along with a distancing from traditional family importance, all contribute to societal descent.

Parenting is critical to the prevention of delinquency and other youth difficulties including violence and abuse. Studies show that single-parent families are potentially more harmful than traditional two-parent homes. According to the report titled *U.S. Single Parent Households*,[5] 85% of children who exhibit behavior disorders, 75% of children in chemical dependency hospitals, and 85% of youths sitting in prisons come from single-parent households.

I will stress however that two-parent homes where no love and true care and compassion exist may be more unhealthy or detrimental than a single-parent home where love and sensitivity are consistently present.

Here Maslow's theory of love and belongingness loom very large. Children have an innate longing for both mom and dad and are more prone to feelings of rejection or abandonment when one or both parents are absent. A sense of not being loved or wanted may arise thus setting in motion a series of later effects which can play out over the course of the lifespan of the individual. Typically, children from single-parent homes are exposed to certain conditions that can increase the probability of delinquency and risk-taking behaviors. These conditions include poorer neighborhoods, parental rejection, and the social responses towards such youths.

Social responses which include that of law enforcement and other public assistance programs may be insensitive to family conditions or needs and can sometimes have negative results. While the primary objective of such social programs is to provide goods and/or services to the community, certain policies and unwritten codes built into their execution, or of the conduct of some of its service providers, may create harmful consequences. Some of these aftereffects could linger for a long time. Many young adults develop criminal behaviors based on outgrowths from adolescent years which may not have provided the nurturing or appropriate parenting necessary to develop proper character or integrity.

Felony and other convictions follow an individual over the course of the person's lifetime and will assist in the management of specific demographic populations by authorities. Groups are lumped together, barring some individuals out of certain job markets and funneling them into other less lucrative ones based on circumstances stemming from early family dysfunction.

People can be shepherded closer together and identified more readily if we develop categories or files in which to place them. Once you have been introduced into this type of system it is simpler to be brought back into the mainstream of corrections management economics. Regarding economics, once again I refer to the creation of jobs, taxes, federal grants and spending money for those considered to be the good citizenry of the community, while the unsavory community members makeup the underclass that are meant to operate in a subservient manner to the more approved class.

Those who are locked out of many of the amenities afforded those considered worthier based on class, credit, and family designations or background, foster animosity among the classes. If we allow our youth to be formed or fashioned in this way we doom them and their children to be cast into the fire of poverty, imprisonment or an underclass lifestyle.

In so doing we allow individuals who are considered to be the approved of class or otherwise designated do develop and maintain a false image of themselves which does much harm to society as a whole.

Those considered middleclass or lower-middleclass look down upon those considered less significant than they, while the middleclass is looked down on by the upper-class. Clearly, all classes serve the ruling-class who may feel or operate in a loftier manner than all other assigned classes. This, too, is a construct and not merely happenstance.

Good police work and staying on top of the overall crime picture is one thing; however, conversely the implementation of a profile registry characterized by socio-economic status or race is questionable to say the least.

I remember when my twins were born. At that time, we already had a three-year-old daughter. Upon the advent of the twin's birth our three-year-old began behaving in a puzzlingly way. She began standing directly in our faces much more frequently. She would say things like, *"Look at this,"* or *"Watch me,"* or *"I can do a summersault," "Look, look!"* She was inwardly feeling that our attention was no longer fixed upon her as the apple of our eye. She needed the affirmation that she would continue to receive our love.

Young people are screaming *"Love me!" "Pay attention to me!"* Do we give fitting consideration to their plea? As in the case of my daughter, she may have felt set aside because of what may have been perceived by her as a replacement. Today's youth may subconsciously feel set to the side by some of our other pursuits. Jobs, enjoyments, relationships, habits, and so many other careers that we engage in, leaving them without our time and attention they cry out, *"Hey, look at me!"* Many of the shocking behaviors that we see in our youth may be nothing more than a roar to be noticed, affirmed and loved. I believe that we can do much to stem the tide of youth crime by first setting aside time for the youth who reside in our own homes.

First and foremost, we must focus on the youth whose lives we have been blessed with as a legacy. We must love them without producing condemnation or a judgmental atmosphere. Guiding and sharing our own hopes, strengths, and testimonies with our youths will instill in them the confidence that comes with belonging to a solid group. If we can produce genuine awareness of the connections among the old, not-so-old, young, and the younger members — as well as the yet unborn of our families, we will be able to develop the funnel through which we can channel unfettered love wrapped in the unity of the family. The story board of our history and the unity of the family unit can then be seen in a linear fashion. This consistent communication being clearly delivered, youth will be much less likely to participate in inappropriate behaviors.

Chapter Four

The Sexuality Reality

Exposure to sexual or other types of abuse increases the risk of delinquency; adolescents exposed to sexual abuse commit about three times more delinquent acts than those not exposed to this form of abuse. According to the National Bureau of Economic Research,[1] *"Child maltreatment roughly doubles the probability that an individual engages in many types of crime. This is true even if we compare twins, one of whom was maltreated when the other one was not."*

Other contrivances can be seen in relation to areas of our lives such as sexuality and misdirected affections. Rarely do things happen exclusively by chance or simply by accident. When societal conditions exist, we must understand that components have painstakingly been put in place to bring about a resulting outcome. But the question we may ask is, *"Put in place by whom?"* In the Book of Ephesians, Chapter Six, Versus 10 through 12, we are told:

"Finally, be strong in the Lord and in His mighty power, put on the full armor of God so that you can take your stand against the devil's schemes. For our struggle is not against flesh and blood, but against the rulers, against the authorities, against the powers of this dark world and against the spiritual forces of evil in the heavenly realms."

Could this be an indication of, or a reason for, many of the ills we see in so many homes and communities today? Are we warring against an unseen foe, but attempting to fight with carnal weaponry? Are we simply attempting to think our way out of what can only be understood and fought against by spiritual methods?

True understanding can only come from the author of the Manual for living on this Earth: The ***B**asic **I**nstruction **B**efore **L**eaving **E**arth* Manual, commonly referred to as the Bible! We must digest its truths to become successful as individuals, families, neighborhoods, communities, cities, states and so on. Grabbing hold of these truths and rigorously teaching them to our youth without recoiling or balking when untoward opposition arises, but remaining resolute in our commitment to bring veracity to the next generation of humankind. We must fully understand that an enemy remains who plants kernels of misleading falsehoods along the way as we journey through history to eternity. He plans on directing the destiny of humanity to meet his treacherous conspiracy. He is determined to manipulate humankind away from the true undertaking our Creator has planned for us.

The *Center for Disease Control and Prevention*[2] reports teen birth rates have risen for the first time in 15 years. Latinas have the highest teen pregnancy rate in the U.S. Between the ages of 15 and 19, Latinas had 81.7 pregnancies per 1,000 girls, while white (non-Hispanic) teens had 25.9 pregnancies per 1,000. Some teen pregnancy counselors blame socio-economic status, lack of education, and inadequate access to contraception for increased teen birth rates.

When we of the baby boom generation were young, kissing and making out was much of what consumed our thoughts and dreams. How to get her to the point where she would say *"Yes"* when asked the all-important question, *"Will you go with me?"* was foremost on the male mind. But that always seemed like an unfinished question to me. Go with me where? It was just a form question to ask the girl if she would be your steady girlfriend, but it just never seemed like a complete question to me. Oh well!

Then if she said *"Yes"* you began the awkward succession of phone calls. You tried to be as private as you could be with all your brothers and sisters around. You tried to keep your mom and dad from interfering or overhearing your conversations by stretching the phone cord to the most secluded spot possible.

Invariably however the phone would be located in the TV room where everyone sat in the evening watching TV. After all the nervousness and discomfort of building up the courage to ask her to go with you, then you had to build up enough bravado to take the initiative to actually lean in to kiss her. This kiss only could take place after the third or fourth date, hoping against all hope that she wouldn't be so shy and turn away and say *"I'm not that kind of girl."*

Back then everybody knew a girl who was considered "easy." She was the girl nobody truly wanted as their prize yet all the guys liked her because she liked to fool around. Guys kissed her and ran their hands all over her body. She would giggle and say *"Stop it, you so nasty."* But her eyes and body language said, *"Do it again."* After spending time with her, boys felt confident with the girl they really wanted to take to the school dance or home to meet the family. When the time and conditions were just right the young man who had fondled the easy chick would then utilize his scientifically formulated method he had perfected. He would then employ those tactics with his real girlfriend. Once they finally did it (kissing or going all the way), he considered himself "The man!"

By contrast, youths today seem to have surpassed our uncertain, hesitant and tentative methods, going immediately straight for the prize. Boys and girls alike! Not to imply that we didn't have sex when we were young because we did. Truth be told, we in the 40-plus set unequivocally had sex as teens and continue to have sex as adults with various partners.

What sets today's youth apart is the *"in your face, here it is"* lack of fear, embarrassment or shame posture. It seems sort of like a badge of honor for young boys to impregnate or at least have sex with as many girls as possible. Girls seem to have the same distain for traditional decorum and modesty as we see 17-year-old girls with three babies by three different males, and they will ask you in a heartbeat *"What you lookin at?"*

We have youths sporting alternate lifestyles brazenly un-abashed; boldly displaying what was once disgraceful and very shameful behavior. Truth is, it's still disgraceful and very shameful behavior, but it's just out there like that and the youths embrace it as OK.

The question that youths seem to have at the ready, almost intrinsically built into their audaciously intrepid demeanor, is, *"What the f--k you gonna do about it?"* I don't know how to answer that question other than, *"Love you through it."* Love you while you're making life choices realizing that the world has us confused too! We are all just trying to understand how to make it to the next day. I'll guide you by demonstration and be there for you no matter what. I'll pray for you, provide for you, and continue to plan with you and for you. I'll share truth with you, and live righteously in your presence to the best of my ability. I'll be honest with you. Through it all I'll trust God. I'll trust God for me and for you that His word in our lives will never fail to produce what it claims. I'll do my part and allow God's word to do His part, thereby demonstrating to you that you can trust the word of God.

Out west an GLBT (Gay, Lesbian, Bisexual, Transgender) organization based in the State of Texas provided information about what they felt the state of affairs were with the youth population that they serve. They were gracious enough to provide the following answers to my questions in a "26 Q and A session:"

Q1. When did you begin working with youth?
A1. In 1989!

Q2. What is your target age group?
A2. Ages 14 through 22!

Q3. In general, what is your impression of today's youth?
A3. Free thinkers; open-minded, creative!

Q4. What would you say their most formidable challenges are?
A4. The biggest challenges for the GLBT population here are acceptance and safety. These are at the root of most every other challenge in their lives.

Q5. What are the most notable successes of today's youth?
A5. Once they come out, they go through a process of self-acceptance that prepares them to excel in the world.

Q6. How do you see adult-youth relations?
A6. The youth we work with are starving for adults who accept them.

Q7. What is the most significant role the schools, churches, home and community play in the overall preparation of youth, and are we meeting needs adequately?
A7. Schools: it depends on the specific school. Most in Texas are not providing a safe and nurturing environment for GLBT youth. It is hard for a youth who does not feel safe to get a decent education. Church: most of the conservative churches are abusive to the GLBT population. They give our youth a skewed image of who God is. Home: provides either a strong sense of acceptance or rejection for the GLBT youth. Community: once our youth find us, they have a sense of belonging and acceptance.

Q8. What impact would you say hip hop has had on today's youth, also the drug culture, and the mainstream media?
A8. Not sure!

Q9. Are single parent homes difficult for youth?
A9. Yes, but I don't find it to be scarring for them.

Q10. Remember the term latch key kids, what if any affect has that had on today's youth?
A10. The lack of supervision, whether latch key or not, allows youth too much freedom. This allows them to get into situations they are not ready or mature enough to handle. The Internet has made this even more evident.

Q11. Do you think that homosexuality has been accepted as a norm with our youth?
A11. It is much better than in years past, but there is still work to be done.

Q12. What about promiscuity?
A12. Accepted, yes! But we have found a new wave of youth who are virgins and proud to be so.

Q13. As parents, what percentage are we responsible for failures and/or successes of our youth?
A13. I don't have an answer.

Q14. Do you think that the economic crisis we face as parents has any impact on our youth?
A14. Yes. Youth can sense parent's stress. It creates an insecure environment. Different youth will respond differently to the stress.

Q15. When I was a kid it was common for families to eat at the table together. Is there any value in that today? If so, what is that value? If not, why is there no value?

A15. I think there is a value in families spending time together. The important aspects of the time include the ability to talk and the feeling that the youth are expected and included.

Q16. Are school systems less or more effective today than they were 30 or 40 years ago?
A16. I don't know!

Q17. Talk a little about the juvenile court system. What are your overall impressions of its effectiveness?
A17. It is overrun and more focused on getting youth off the streets than in treatment. It is totally unprepared to work with GLBT youth.

Q18. What about adult court systems?
A18. Ineffective!

Q19. I have heard youth as well as adults say *"F--k the police."* Why do you think so many today have that perspective?
A19. We have become a society in which we don't trust the police any longer. We see so much on TV about corruption and misuse of power. It is difficult to give over our power to an unknown person just because they wear a police uniform.

Q20. I have been in households where the kids make their own rules. How does this exist?
A20. The parents have given into the belief that success equals money and things. Their priorities are not in order.

Q21. What can parents do to maintain healthy relations with their children?
A21. Spend time, give attention, and get to know them instead of try to form or mold them.

Q22. What can communities do to maintain healthy relations with its children?

A22. Provide a safe environment where youth can grow to be who they are without fear. Provide a variety of activities so youth will stay interested and challenged.

Q23. Talk a little about religion and youth.
A23. Adolescent years are a time to explore beliefs and values. A religion that allows questions and investigation is more likely to attract and keep youth. Religions that are fear-based, exclusionary and dictatorial are less likely to do so. Our population of youth is less likely to be involved in religion because so many reject them and tell them they are going to hell for being who they are.

Q24. If we followed cause and effect, what would be the cause that shows us the effect we see in today's youth?
24. I don't have an answer.

Q25. Tell me about one of the greatest success stories of your organization?
A25. To see a youth come to us insecure, unsure and filled with self-hatred, yet in a short time feel accepted for who they are. The growth and change is almost tangible. Our success relies on an environment of unconditional acceptance.

Q26. If you could give a gift to our youth what would it be?
A26. An environment that celebrates diversity!

The previous interview was indeed conducted with a youth homosexuality community based organization located in the south western portion of the country. By virtue of the fact that gender confusion is taking place at the current pace today, obviously something is materializing that must be examined more closely. Young individuals embraced in affirming communities which provide guidance and leadership of youthful minds is typically a positive factor in societies. However, cementing flawed identities further into the confused minds of youths and fostering acceptance of distorted self-perceptions beg certain questions to be answered.

Sidebar: *If I am on the edge of going down a steep slope from which I have not the wherewithal or desire to halt my descent, and someone I trust tells me to keep going, if I do follow, will we not both be injured when ultimately, we fall off the cliff side?*

Now don't take this the wrong way! I cannot or do not presume to judge anyone; my house is made of glass also, therefore I throw no stones. I have however lived long enough to see the progression and promotion of various lifestyles and the deterioration of others. I remember "Boy meets girl!" I remember customary gender identity.

And now the line is so obscured that we must ask ourselves what happened, and if we continue along the present path, what could the world be like 40 years into the future?

Androgyny in so many of our music icons has become all too common. The passing of Michael Jackson brought about national and world sadness. Admittedly due to his untimely demise, I feel the loss of one of my familiar musical voices and faces. I love M.J.'s music and admired his talent and creative genius. However, there is no ambiguity or vagueness about the fact that the softness of his speaking voice and his feminine hairstyle with no overt male features, has been not only accepted but promoted and emulated by many before as well as after Michael.

Many others in the public eye also present themselves in this fashion. Many in modern society wittingly or unwittingly take their cues on how to dress and behave from Hollywood creations.

I would suppose that homosexuality and gender bending has existed for as long as people have been on this Earth. The account given about the unbridled sexual activities in Sodom and Gomorrah is ancient history. It provides us with a look into the longstanding nature of these activities as well as God's displeasure with people succumbing to such tendencies.

Everyone has a struggle with certain tendencies or temptations, but to the one who overcomes, that one shall be saved according to the Manual. If my temptation is tobacco or overeating, lying, drugs or stealing, I must fight the good fight and overcome it and not allow it to take me captive.

All sin is sin! I don't see one sin as having more stature than another sin. We have all sinned and fallen short of the glory of God in one way or another. Even if it's just being born in sin, we are found sinful and have need of the Savior.

However, at some point in our development as a race of human beings we eventually should get our own personal struggles righted. One by one we must seek truth and yield our prideful will to the authority of the Lord. Only then will our communities develop the kind of character it takes to instill a greater measure of decency. By continuing such a course, ultimately, we gain strength as a society. We would then be able to see the testimony of others who overcame and follow their good example instead of following the poorer examples of the defeated and the fallen.

Similarly, alcohol and other drug addictions, obsessive gambling, over eating, and so many other life distractions require the same attention and redirection. Admittedly, I do not have the answers to these questions. One thing however is true and factual; if all mankind without exception practiced homosexuality exclusively, mankind would not exist after just a few generations; therefore, outside of any moral question, clearly there is an inherent danger here that must be examined.

As with other questions in this book, I leave the deliberation with you. You can look inside yourself; explore your past and your environment and answer to the best of your ability the questions set before us all. At some point, we must come to a resolute consensus on questions of ethics and moral conduct. As the saying goes, *"If we stand for nothing we will fall for anything."* We must ask ourselves the hard questions and be inwardly honest and stalwart enough to answer with conviction and stay our determined course. The difficulty in making the tough decisions and sticking with our decided upon course must be challenged and overcome.

We must recognize that as the human race, we are one family! It is essential that we do the things necessary to maintain — as well as enhance — our relations with our family members. The line in the sand is being drawn; sides are being selected and the big dance is being prepared to take place.

When you were a kid and a pickup game of baseball or kickball was getting ready to commence, you selected sides. Or maybe you were preparing to play "Hide-and-go-seek" and the person to be "it" had to be selected. Most likely you had a devised method of choosing the person to be "it." We had to determine who was on this team and who was on the other team. As for us we all put our foot in the circle and the caller said something like, *"Dishy dishy ice cream dishy dishy out!"* We whittled it down to the last foot in the circle and that person was "it."

Or you may have had two captains pick one person each at a time until everyone was assigned a team. Similarly, on a global scale we are picking up teams. There is a team of darkness and a team of light. Which side will you choose for yourself and your family? Will sin, crime, despair, greed, lust and perversion really win most of us to play on its team? Will the sides be uneven? What about the side of truth and righteousness, will many choose that side? Not the brand of truth and righteousness that we rationalize ourselves into believing is standard, but the brand set forth by the writer of the owner's Manual for living here on Earth.

Are there more players on the opposing team than on the team of righteousness, truth, honesty, fairness and godliness? Either wittingly or unwittingly we choose. Maybe it's by deception or even with eyes wide shut; we still choose. It's clear there is no middle ground; a little leaven leavens the whole lump. We are all together in our families, communities, cities, states, this nation, and indeed, the world. What I ingest into the smallest part of my body affects me entirely. We all inhale the same air and a little air pollution any place in the world eventually gets into every one's lungs. If one, one hundredth percent of cyanide was put in a gallon of fresh drinking water, would you feel comfortable drinking it? Why is it that we look on while our brother's and sister's hearts and minds are polluted, and act as if we ourselves will not eventually be affected?

Sound rationale and the foundational principles supporting them must be presented to our future generations at all cost by those of us who are in custodial positions. It is not necessarily parents alone who are responsible for their own child and that's all. We are all responsible for all youth! What about the upcoming generations and the present community as a whole? We are all liable agents of care for all youth and the future of humanity. As the saying goes, it takes an entire village to raise a child. I would go further and say that it takes a world to raise a child; at the very least it takes a nation.

I am officially going on record as one who apologizes to my own children, as well as to the younger generation as a whole, for my portion in assisting in the dismantling of the valid culture in which we were intended by God to live. I have played a part in helping society descend to the extent we see today. I also am not exempt from responsibility for the scratches, dents and dings that are presently on display in the body work of the culture of today. Moreover, for the "under the hood damage" which causes the real breakdowns, I apologize. The fresh paint that was at one time in the distant past without blemish has become weather-beaten and worn-looking, due in part, to my carelessness, and I am sorry for the part that I had in it and ask you for your forgiveness.

I am not the only one culpable, but I can only clean my own front porch. Will you yourself recognize and acknowledge this and make the necessary resolve to begin anew with a determination to prepare today's youth for great future accomplishments? Not only am I referring to the preparation of your own child, but an entire generation of champions who, in turn, will produce a whole new generation of victorious, overcomers. Just think of what the world would be like in 40 more years if we all resolved to make the necessary realignments now which can lead to a refreshed generation of true future captains.

Imagine if you will a current that you and your spouse find yourselves caught in with no other way to negotiate it other than to swim upstream. The force of the stream is beating so vehemently against you that making headway is most often impossible. Once you manage to find one you hold on to a boulder protruding out of the water. With all your might you hang on only to find that you must let go and reaffirm your grasp on the rock just a little distance behind your previous position because of the ferocity of the current. Albeit behind the position you previously held, you cling on with all your might. The stream is unrelenting and beats against you mercilessly. Day after disenchanted day, week after weary week, year upon lingering year you hold on and let go to reaffirm your hold.

The force of the current never stops beating you back, little by little. This becomes life as you know it; it's all you can do just to stay afloat. You manage to have children and they in turn have offspring of their own, all the while generations move further downstream. Generation after generation, life goes on long after you and your spouse's demise. The present generation having no knowledge of your former position far upstream, believing from their shortsighted view that the rock they presently hold is all there is or should be, After all, *"We are holding fast with all the vigor at our disposal,"* they declare!

But while paddling to beat the band just to stay the status quo, never looking just a few generations downstream from the present standing to recognize that there is a very long drop off the water's edge boasting foreboding consequences. While taking no real appraisal of the fact that without divine intervention certain doom is imminent; they trudge onward.

I submit to you today that we are looming very close to the water fall that could have calamitous results for tomorrow's world and its populous cities and nations. The world which will be populated by our children, grandchildren and their offspring is at stake. Do we truly care about their plight? After all, most of us may be long gone by the time the plunge over the edge is taken. Can we care enough to provide not only the money making and technological advancements they'll need, but also the moral and ethical tools needed to build a better floatation device in which our future's youth can sail away from the consuming waterfall awaiting them?

Additionally, can we provide enough love, compassion, understanding and unselfish demonstration of Godly restoration from the halls of our court rooms, to the seats of our classrooms? Can we transport our youth from someone's plushy bedroom back to the plushy cushions of our own living rooms? It is there where we can participate in meaningful dialogue first; yes, in our homes with our young, providing them with structure, direction, unconditional love and an accurate road map leading to the long sought after but elusive oasis of rest.

Only then shall tomorrow's generation of capable treasures be able to branch out into their world, finding their true destiny. Holistically we digressed; we must by the same measure or even greater measure approach this topic in order to progress from every facet of community life. Of necessity we must restore family to its former glory and communal significance.

Crime and violence has become a main staple in the dietary makeup of our youth's spiritual intake. We see it in our streets, in our schools, and on our movie and TV screens. More fore-bodingly we see crime and violence in our homes much too often. Is there a better regiment of more healthy consumables that we can provide to supplement this poor intake habit?

How about some "peaceful peas" and "unruffled red apples?" Maybe one could digest some "nonmilitant mangos" or "passionate passionfruit" or perhaps some "jackfruit joy." Dig some "Indian freedom figs" or "abstinent May apples." What about chowing down on some "wakame wait," "Godly golden samphires," or some "sweet pepper smarts?" Always good this time of year is the "saskatoon study," "peaceful persimmon," "friendly figs," or some "truthful tomatillos" or its equivalent, the "Tigernut truth." The "anti-gross-out azuki bean," or of course the "anti-nerd naranja" and the "anti-geek gherkin" may also be served. These are all good diets for prevention and maintenance of healthy attitudes, character and self-esteem.

These are linked with social or ethical issues in hopes that consuming these healthier items will foster greater cooperation between generations and produce less violence and crime in the lives of those who employ what they imply. Self-control is an essential part of what is needed in order that we comply with the mandate set forth in the Manual. As the present adult population, we must not simply shake our head in displeasure at what we see our youth doing but by demonstration prove a better way.

Understanding that we all have needs and desires as well as remembering when we were youthful doesn't justify continuation of detrimental practices. In many ways, we sanction poor behavior by our youth by practicing the same things ourselves. Having sexual relationships as unmarried youths can and often does hinder growth potential; it produces unwanted pregnancies and so many other life complications. As leaders and teachers in our homes and communities we must lead by proper example. We must first get out of the compromising positions that we are in and demonstrate character and integrity. I cannot impress upon the children in my community that premarital sex is inappropriate while having premarital or extramarital affairs myself. As an example, I must clean my own front porch first and allow others to see the value of virtue in action.

Chapter Five

On The Record

I am a person who enjoys sports very much. I played line-backer on my high school football team. I still see my coach around the city from time to time. He was forceful and very animated. He taught me a lot about football and a lot about life. The experience of being on the team and gaining all the friendships and life lessons helped to shape character. I learned a lot about getting along with others and working together for a common goal. These principles remain with me today.

I was a smaller person than many of the other players. I was rather thin and not very fast but I had heart and tenacity. One day during practice, coach paced back and forth as he monitored the drills we were going through on this hot summer day. We sizzled on the practice field where we spent hours sweating in the heat of the sweltering midday sun. He was a rather large man. Not fat but muscular with massive thighs, a powerful chest and shoulders along with a strong torso. He was somewhat of a celebrity around town because he had played on the college level at the university in the city where I grew up; he got much respect. As he paced up and down the rows he sharply blew his whistle — which was the command for us to drop swiftly to the ground, and even more hurriedly get back up and continue running in place.

I saw him coming down the row near me and I fully expected him to keep walking right on past. However, he stopped in front of me and looked intently at me, sort of sizing me up with his piercing eyes and confrontational scowl. He sucked in his gut squared his shoulders, flared his nostrils and bellowed, *"Look at that turkey neck,"* referring to my skinny neck. That statement embarrassed me so; I didn't measure up. Instantly I felt that I was less than him and the other players and needed something I didn't have. I felt that obviously I was less than the other guys too because he didn't stop to devalue them. What was to be done with that load that he dropped in my lap? How could I fit the expectation of my coach that I respected so much? Now, whether real or just in my mind, the entire team now must view me as less than they are because of the statement made by my coach!

Maybe his remark was meant to toughen me up somehow. Could he have known if I had some self-esteem issues already at work? Could he have known whether his comment would be received in the vein in which I'm sure it was given, or if I would be dashed to the jagged rocks below? How could he know?

Why did he say that in front of everybody? After witnessing the homemade riots at our house as a kid and hearing insulting missiles fired one after another, sometimes the trajectory of those Weapons of Mass Destruction were aimed at me and they hit the target dead on the bull's-eye on a regular basis. I was already setup to receive coach's comment negatively.

After a few more weeks of practice, post turkey neck comment, I just didn't come back to play on the team that year. I had internalized and magnified the coach's comment to the extent that I felt unworthy of being on the team and I was somewhat ashamed and embarrassed. Right or wrong that's what happened. I opted out. You may say that I was a quitter and all the coach was doing was attempting to point out to me what I needed to do to improve my chances of being successful as a football player.

The fact is, I felt powerless to be the kind of person that he was telling me that I needed to become, at least at that time. Much to my discredit, in the presence of his authority and celebrity, I shank! The way I felt about myself and the life lessons I had come to understand at that time was all I could pull from to make my decision.

I lingered in the moment long after the coach, and probably after everyone else had forgotten any such comment. He did not give me positive reinforcement. He didn't give me instruction on how to change what he saw as a negative to my becoming a successful football player. He just provided me with a simple ridicule. That simple statement blossomed into a much larger image that may have partnered with any number of other preexisting statements or events that may have changed my future forever. We must take care in the way we speak to your youth.

Let's say that I was encouraged and nurtured as a player and I didn't quit the football team, but instead continued to play. Over time became very good and received a college scholarship, was well educated in a specific area of science, and ultimately came to develop something that was instrumental in the cure for cancer.

Or let's say that I continued to play football, and as a senior broke my leg. While in the hospital I met a candy strip girl who became the love of my life. We married, and as a result of our union she gave birth to a child that became president of the United States of America. Perhaps I ultimately became a member of a world Super Bowl championship team, made millions and created a great philanthropic foundation dedicated to improving young minds. There are many imaginings that could be employed here. While all of this is simply conjecture on my part, it's real in the sense that circumstances alter the paths that our lives take. It is a very sensitive balance which develops environments which can spring youths forward or create atmospheric conditions which can spiral down a life into a tailspin of defeat. As adults, we must handle the fragile lives of our youth with care and tenderness. We do not know or understand any preexisting maladies which may be at work in the delicate emotional mind of an individual.

There are many ways in which youthful minds seek attention. Attention of the opposite sex is usually a primary focus. Playing on the sports teams was a big way to gain the girls attention in my school days. There are many other avenues which one might take to become more attractive, with the goal of being loved, admired, affirmed, cared for, or simply just being noticed. Look into your own past, review how you made yourself as desirable as you could to gain entry onto the social playing field. Once in the arena it felt like somebody took a can opener and opened up what had been sealed so tightly inside. In some areas, once the can is opened the contents can't stay in the container any longer; neither can you reseal it. So be careful what you allow to be opened in your life. Be very careful when you allow areas of your life to be opened, and probably most importantly be careful of who is found holding your can opener.

Some say life is just a complex assortment of decisions. We live, have experiences and experiments from which we learn and grow. Our experiences and choices are quantifiably impacted by those around us. Life experiences influenced by the atmosphere of the world we grow up in as a young person is very impactful. The world at large and our personal world along with our predisposed tendencies all played a part in molding us into who we ultimately become.

Thunder & Lightning: A Storm Is Coming

Admittedly I made mistakes along the way as I made attempt after agonizing attempt to understand my world and how I fit into it. To illustrate how generational we are as a society let's look back. For those of us who can't recollect what life in the 1960s was like for Americans during that very transformative period of rebellious idealism, let me refresh your memory. Allow me to digress a bit here as I reminisce on those times. Prior to the 1950s we had a nation which had just come out of the devastation of World War II.

In a Tom Brokaw special on the era of the 1960s, Theodore Roszak, a Cal State Professor of history, stated that, *"Parents of the 50s were, I think, the most unusual generation of the 20th century in the world. They had just come out of the depression and the trauma of the war. They experienced tough times when they were children and teens, then World War II hit as many of them were just reaching adulthood, and they had the trauma of the war, and after all that they reached the 50s at a time when the United States was tremendously prosperous, when the economy was booming as we never seen it before. And I think they reacted to the prosperity and reacted strongly to all that trauma of the war by turning inward a bit by marrying young by emphasizing home and family as if that was something they couldn't get back in the 30s and 40s, and was valued all the more."*

In the 1960s we had the civil rights movement setting a backdrop of unrest, and uneasiness about relationships between races and even members within the same race could feel much heat from one another. Topics such as abortion rights, civil rights, women's rights, pollution, politics, as well as police brutality, blazed across the headlines and onto our hearts and minds.

There were impressive individuals on both sides of the civil rights movement passionately in conflict in support of their positions. In June 1963, George Wallace blocked the enrollment of African American students, Malone and Hood at the University of Alabama. Similar actions in Birmingham, Huntsville, and Mobile made him a national figure and he was one of the country's leading figures against the civil rights movement.

In February 1968, Wallace announced his intention of standing as an independent candidate for president. His hostility to civil rights legislation won him support from white voters in the Deep South and won him Arkansas, Louisiana, Mississippi, Alabama and Georgia. Here are two famous quotes from Quotesdaddy.com[1] that have been attributed to Mr. Wallace: *"If any demonstrator ever lies down in front of my car, it'll be the last car he'll ever lay down in front of."* And, *"I draw the line in the dust and toss the gauntlet before the feet of tyranny, and I say segregation now, segregation tomorrow, segregation forever."*

Another outspoken opponent of civil rights for all Americans was David Duke,[2] who is attributed with the following quote: *"Our clear goal must be the advancement of the white race and separation of the white and black races. This goal must include freeing of the American media and government from subservient Jewish interests."*

From the 1880s into the 1960s, a majority of American states enforced segregation through "Jim Crow" laws (so called after a black character in minstrel shows). From Delaware to California, and from North Dakota to Texas, many states (and cities, too) could impose legal punishments on people for consorting with members of another race. The most common types of laws forbade intermarriage and ordered business owners and public institutions to keep their black and white clientele separated. Here is a sampling of such laws from various states, based on public records:

Buses: All passenger stations in this state operated by any motor transportation company shall have separate waiting rooms or spaces and separate ticket windows for the white and colored races. *Alabama*

Railroads: The conductor of each passenger train is authorized and required to assign each passenger to the car or the division of the car, when it is divided by a partition, designated for the race to which such passenger belongs. *Alabama*

Restaurants: It shall be unlawful to conduct a restaurant or other place for the serving of food in the city, at which white and colored people are served in the same room, unless such white and colored persons are effectually separated by a solid partition extending from the floor upward to a distance of seven feet or higher, and unless a separate entrance from the street is provided for each compartment. *Alabama*

Sidebar: As a youth I went with my family to Mississippi for the funeral of an aunt. While there we went to a restaurant counter to get a bite to eat. As we stepped to the counter to place our order the clerk (a Caucasian woman) ignored the fact that we were there; she pretended to be wiping the counter top. I spoke up to insist on ordering but my parents, who are from the South, told me hush, hush just wait. I couldn't understand that at all. The clerks disregard for us and my parent's cooperation with it was rather odd, I thought. But my parents understood something that I did not: Jim Crow!

Toilet Facilities, Male: Every employer of white and Negro males shall provide for such white or Negro males reasonably accessible and separate toilet facilities. *Alabama*

Intermarriage: The marriage of a person of Caucasian blood with a Negro, Mongolian, Malay, or Hindu shall be null and void. *Arizona*

Intermarriage: All marriages between a white person and a Negro, or between a white person and a person of Negro descent to the fourth generation inclusive, are hereby forever prohibited. *Florida*

Cohabitation: Any Negro man and white woman, or any white man and Negro woman, who are not married to each other, who shall habitually live in and occupy in the nighttime the same room shall each be punished by imprisonment not exceeding twelve (12) months, or by fine not exceeding five hundred ($500.00) dollars. *Florida*

Education: The schools for white children and the schools for Negro children shall be conducted separately. *Florida*

Burial: The officer in charge shall not bury, or allow to be buried, any colored persons upon ground set apart or used for the burial of white persons. *Georgia*

Amateur Baseball: It shall be unlawful for any amateur white baseball team to play baseball on any vacant lot or baseball diamond within two blocks of a playground devoted to the Negro race, and it shall be unlawful for any amateur colored baseball team to play baseball in any vacant lot or baseball diamond within two blocks of any playground devoted to the white race. *Georgia*

Parks: It shall be unlawful for colored people to frequent any park owned or maintained by the city for the benefit, use and enjoyment of white persons...and unlawful for any white person to frequent any park owned or maintained by the city for the use and benefit of colored persons. *Georgia*

Housing: Any person...who shall rent any part of any such building to a Negro person or a Negro family when such building is already in whole or in part in occupancy by a white person or white family, or vice versa when the building is in occupancy by a Negro person or Negro family, shall be guilty of a misdemeanor and on conviction thereof shall be punished by a fine of not less than twenty-five ($25.00) nor more than one hundred ($100.00) dollars or be imprisoned not less than 10, or more than 60 days, or both such fine and imprisonment in the discretion of the court. *Louisiana*

Promotion of Equality: Any person...who shall be guilty of printing, publishing or circulating printed, typewritten or written matter urging or presenting for public acceptance or general information, arguments or suggestions in favor of social equality or of intermarriage between whites and Negroes, shall be guilty of a misdemeanor and subject to fine of not exceeding five hundred (500.00) dollars or imprisonment not exceeding six (6) months or both. *Mississippi*

Prisons: The warden shall see that the white convicts shall have separate apartments for both eating and sleeping from the Negro convicts. *Mississippi*

Textbooks: Books shall not be interchangeable between the white and colored schools, but shall continue to be used by the race first using them. *North Carolina*

Libraries: The state librarian is directed to fit up and maintain a separate place for the use of the colored people who may come to the library for the purpose of reading books or periodicals. *North Carolina*

Transportation: The...Utilities Commission...is empowered and directed to require the establishment of separate waiting rooms at all stations for the white and colored races. *North Carolina*

Teaching: Any instructor who shall teach in any school, college or institution where members of the white and colored race are received and enrolled as pupils for instruction shall be deemed guilty of a misdemeanor, and upon conviction thereof, shall be fined in any sum not less than ten dollars ($10.00) nor more than fifty dollars ($50.00) for each offense. *Oklahoma*

Fishing, Boating, and Bathing: The Conservation Commission shall have the right to make segregation of the white and colored races as to the exercise of rights of fishing, boating and bathing. *Oklahoma*

Mining: The baths and lockers for the Negroes shall be separate from the white race, but may be in the same building. *Oklahoma*

Lunch Counters: No persons, firms, or corporations, who or which furnish meals to passengers at station restaurants or station eating houses, in times limited by common carriers of said passengers, shall furnish said meals to white and colored passengers in the same room, or at the same table, or at the same counter. *South Carolina*

Theaters: Every person...operating...any public hall, theatre, opera house, motion picture show or any place of public entertainment or public assemblage which is attended by both white and colored persons, shall separate the white race and the colored race and shall set apart and designate...certain seats therein to be occupied by white persons and a portion thereof, or certain seats therein, to be occupied by colored persons. *Virginia*

Living with such an undercurrent of built-in, institutionalized, racial inequality required courageous voices to speak out, to expose the anguish set upon them by the oppressive nature of racism. Voices such as those of Martin Luther King, Jr. and Malcolm X were perhaps the two most prominent voices of resistance to the oppression of racism. There were many, many others who voiced opposition in the 1950s and 1960s, some black and some white.

The resounding voice of Dr. Martin Luther King, Jr. proclaimed, *"I believe that unarmed truth and unconditional love will have the final word in reality. That is why right, temporarily defeated, is stronger than evil triumphant."*

Secondly, Dr. King said, *"Like an unchecked cancer, hate corrodes the personality and eats away its vital unity. Hate destroys a man's sense of values and his objectivity. It causes him to describe the beautiful as ugly and the ugly as beautiful, and to confuse the true with the false and the false with the true."*

Thirdly, Dr. King stated that, *"Segregation is the adultery of an illicit intercourse between injustice and immorality."* (Source of the above three Dr. King quotes: Quotationpage.com*)*

Malcolm X is quoted as saying: *"We declare our right on this Earth...to be a human being, to be respected as a human being, to be given the rights of a human being in this society, on this Earth, in this day, which we intend to bring into existence by any means necessary."*

And the following quote by Malcolm X, which is close to the rationale for this book in my thinking, speaks not to black youth or white youth, Asian or Hispanic youth or any other demo-graphic group alone but is all inclusive:

"Look at yourselves. Some of you teenagers, students! How do you think I feel and I belong to a generation ahead of you — how do you think I feel to have to tell you, 'We, my generation, sat around like a knot on a wall while the whole world was fighting for its human rights — and you've got to be born into a society where you still have that same fight.' What did we do,

who preceded you? I'll tell you what we did, nothing. And don't you make the same mistake we made...." — Malcolm X

Malcolm X is also attributed with saying: *"If you've studied the captives being caught by the American soldiers in South Vietnam, you'll find that these guerrillas are young people. Some of them are just children and some haven't reached their teens. Most are teenagers. It is the teenagers abroad, all over the world, who are actually involving themselves in the struggle to eliminate oppression and exploitation. In the Congo, the refugees point out that many of the Congolese revolutionaries, they shoot all the way down to seven years old — that's been reported in the press. Because the revolutionaries are children, young people! In these countries, the young people are the ones who most quickly identify with the struggle and the necessity to eliminate the evil conditions that exist. And here in this country, it has been my own observation that when you get into a conversation on racism and discrimination and segregation, you will find young people more incensed over it — they feel more filled with an urge to eliminate it."*

While a young person myself, there was something so surreal about the black and white images coming through the TV set as I watched the dogs being ordered to attack black protesters as they demonstrated for equality. There were high power water hoses pinning individuals to the front of buildings or knocking them to the ground. I saw angry crowds striking individuals with fists, rocks, and bottles, simply because they wanted fair treatment and to be allowed to live peacefully within their rights afforded under the United States Constitution.

In between the times of seeing these horrific, captivating, almost mind-numbing emotionally supercharged images, mom regularly took us to church and we learned to sing, "*Jesus loves the little children, all the children of the world, red and yellow, black and white, they're all precious in his sight. Jesus loves the little children of the world."*

There in the church hung a picture of a Caucasian depiction of what Jesus was portrayed to look like, with blond hair and blue eyes. The picture looked a lot like the images of those mistreating the people who looked like me. I was one of the children of the world! Did this Jesus really love me? I sometimes wondered. I was somewhat apprehended by the perplexing fact that there in front of me was the indication that our Lord is associated with the very image of that which oppressed us as a race. In light of these realities the statement *"God can do all things and what He has done for others He will do for you,"* just somehow didn't ring as spot on correct. While my belief in God through Christ was then and remains intact, my reality as an African American in this country consistently spoke that I was not as worthy as my non-African American counterparts.

I never doubted for one second and I still unequivocally believe that Jesus does paint all with the same paint stroke of love and all are welcome to come to Him. *"Come unto me all who are burdened and heavy laden and I will give you rest"* He says (Matthew 11:28). I also understand that He is not the likeness of images He is regularly portrayed as in so many portraits. That is not the topic of discussion right now, but clearly something is incongruent here.

However, as a young impressionable mind I needed to make sense of the world. Was the God for me, the same God of the people who were treating me with such loathing? Was the God we worshiped when we went to church where the parishioners were black, the same God as the white church goers worshiped? Was Jim Crow in effect at church too? Well, yeah!

We were totally racially separated in churches on Sundays as we worshiped as if *"God don't allow no mixin!"* Why did we receive such harsh treatment just for wearing brown skin? Many questions from this young mind, but few if any real answers followed.

This was a time of self-awareness and discovery for me as well as our nation. I saw what was being offered to American citizens yet I lived a very different reality. I watched the Nelson boys on *The Adventures of Ozzie and Harriet*, and *Leave it to Beaver* on TV. The static portrayals of family life with dad sitting at the dinner table fully dressed in a tie and jacket, and mom with pearl beads around her neck, high heels on and not a hair out of place, clad in her petite apron over her crispy dress while she makes the meal for her men. A fantasy for sure! A pipe dream! While suburbia was in full swing, I don't imagine life was quite like it was portrayed on those TV programs. And it certainly wasn't like that at our house!

I watched those shows and others like them. I enjoyed them very much. Unfortunately, I perceived by the striking contrast between them and our urban neighborhood conditions in clear and understandable language that the sort of lifestyle displayed on the screen was a phantom. If available to anyone at all it wasn't us down on the east side.

However, I dared to believe that I could have the kind of life in which my needs are met. I knew my children will be cared for, and I can have an up-to-date transportation vehicle, a good job with the kind of benefits that are useful, and a loving wife. But is that all that life is to be? I always envisioned more. I believed God who said that He would give me the desire of my heart if I delighted myself in Him. But my desire and my reality were very dissimilar. Even though I was a young boy and had nothing then, I still looked forward to better days ahead.

My father was a man who handled his financial affairs well. Dad did alright on the small amount he made as an hourly wage earner at a factory job where the work was hard and the hours were long and the pay was very, very poor. My father managed to purchase a new car nearly every three years. My father bought the home that we were raised in and furnished it well. We were provided school clothes and we also ate well. Contemplating on these times when my thoughts and self-images were being nurtured with a lot of input from national affairs, I must admit life got sort of confusing.

Home, community, and national life being such as it was gave thrust to my perceptions of who I was and where I fit in all of this. Notwithstanding my spiritual beliefs added a dimension which really didn't clear the path much wider. Our parents always taught us that we are just as good as anyone else. At church we heard about the love of God, yet our reality remained hard pressed by comparison. This resulted in a lot of soul searching and introspection, a sort of search for truth. Where does this piece of the puzzle fit? This seemed to be the overarching question of my youth. For me it was sort of an elusive equation requiring experimentation with different formulas.

The conflicting, almost subliminal message, the unspoken reality behind the apparent presentation of a truth, was that my skin color mattered to those in positions of control in those days. It may or may not have been a determining barrier to my living in the better neighborhoods, having the better jobs, or receiving the best education. But being respected simply because I am a person on the Earth just like everyone else created by God was somehow strangely elusive in many instances. It became more of a mind fence behind which I allowed myself to remain far too long, testing each inch of the enclosure for the gate that didn't seem to exist. To get out of it I had to resolve to tear the fence down.

At the tender age that I was during the times of the 1960s, it was easy to become impressed by everything going on around me from a national or worldwide perspective. I was 11 years old in 1968.

During that singularly extraordinary year many of my beliefs and perceptions of who I was and how I fit into the world were molded, then torn down and reshaped, then crushed again and re-hung as on a wind chime. I suppose this would explain why each time the winds of adversity blew, all my life clanged in disharmonious jangling.

This was my world, my government, my structured realm in which I had been installed as a participant and I had to correspond and relate accordingly to the set rules, or did I?

I didn't want to just be another individual who lived and died, and that was it. It always felt like there is so much more to life that I was missing. God truly does have a plan and a purpose for us all. Each one of us plays a part in the evolution of creation. I needed to be a part of His plan, but there appeared so much debris between me and this destiny that it almost seemed hopeless to pursue it.

Patrick J. Buchanan, a former Nixon speech writer and presidential hopeful, is quoted as saying of the year 1968: "*It was the culmination of a sexual, civil rights and anti-war revolution in America. I cannot think of a year in American history that was more divisive.*"

One of my personal favorite heroes, Muhammad Ali, refused induction into the military draft, vowing not to go to Vietnam and kill individuals he did not know nor was he harmed by, and do so for individuals he did know and understood them to be his oppressors and adversaries; sadly, his own countrymen.

Muhammad Ali said, *"I ain't draft dodging. I ain't burning no flag. I ain't running to Canada. I'm staying right here. You want to send me to jail? Fine, you go right ahead. I've been in jail for 400 years. I could be there for four or five more, but I ain't going no 10,000 miles to help murder and kill other poor people. If I want to die, I'll die right here, right now, fightin' you, if I want to die. You my enemy, not no Chinese, no Vietcong, no Japanese. You my opposer when I want freedom. You my opposer when I want justice. You my opposer when I want equality. Want me to go somewhere and fight for you? You won't even stand up for me right here in America, for my rights and my religious beliefs. You won't even stand up for my rights here at home."*

The Vietnam War is indelibly etched in my memory. I never served but I saw enough of it. I saw the war fought on TV and I saw it fought right here in our streets and on our college campuses. I saw the war fought on the Six O'clock News each evening for years between pro and con pundits. I heard the war fought in our music by many of the music icons of that era. Songs like, "Blowin' In The Wind," Bob Dylan (1963); "The Willing Conscript," Tom Paxton (1963): "I Ain't Marching Any More," Phil Ochs (1964); "Universal Soldier," Buffy Sainte-Marie (1962); "Eve of Destruction," P. F. Sloan (1965); and "With God on Our Side," Bob Dylan (1963). Jimmy Hendricks and so many more artists fought the war in their music. Protest songs and protest marches with the slogans to go with them, such as, *HELL NO – WE WON'T GO,* became almost like an anthem of sorts with revolutionists and protestors. In 1968 more soldiers died than at any previous time in the war. The body count swelled to an alarming 16,500 dead that year alone.

Many individuals were heading to Canada to avoid going to what was largely considered an unjust war. An American Army Sergeant of the Iraqi War left to live in Canada proclaiming *"I believed what they were saying about the stockpiles of weapons of mass destruction. I believed that this was justification to go to war so I went to war. Then I learned that they had sent me and hundreds of thousands of others to war for a lie."*

I believe that many would-be soldiers of the 1960s may have felt that way as well. How do you imagine many of those soldiers in Vietnam felt when fighting in the quagmire of an unwinnable war, only to eventually come home to a less than receptive American society?

Sidebar: *Archie and the Meathead constantly at odds about the war and everything else for that matter from politics to babies was a true-to-life happening at that time in the lives of many individuals. Family structure began changing, father and son, and mother and daughter disagreements became more frequent and more severe. Politics and lifestyle differences entered the home setting with explosive results.*

Another prospective soldier who fled to Canada from the military draft during the Vietnam era when asked if he felt that he was running out on his country answered, *"America has gone so far warped that she's run out on herself."*

A counterculture revolution began to emerge with "love-ins," "turn-ons, tune-ins, and dropouts." One 60s hippie was noted as saying that *"the total point of love-ins was to be completely opposite of war and killing, to reinvent civilization."*

Music began to take on a psychedelic, harder edge, with musicians like Jimmy Hendricks, Janis Joplin, and Jim Morrison of the Doors, all who not only were well-known drug abusers but also died as a result of their drug use. The drug explosion hit with devastating force in the 1960s. The list of those who met with similar drug induced deaths goes on ad infinitum. The drug use, free love and anti-war revolution was full-blown during these times and it was almost impossible to be unaffected by it in one form or another.

As we watched TV and talked with acquaintances about current events during those times, it had an effect on the entire generation. Not to say that everyone was impacted to their detriment, because obviously everyone was not irrevocably harmed. But there was no way that one could have lived through those turbulent times completely isolated and completely unaffected.

Can you visualize a person traveling on a path and suddenly a mountain lion jumps out and chases him through a tunnel, then down a sharp mountain side? Then he had to stop and fight for his life for 30 minutes. Following this battle, he crossed the river and traveled through an unknown valley. After that he had to climb up a cliff side to safety? Now bloody, battered, and exhausted, he finds himself in a place nowhere near the location the chase began, but he is safe now and must resume his hike from this altered position. Albeit he is resilient and will pick up from here, there is no way this person would be unaffected by such a trauma. When he sleeps he wonders if the lion is near so he changes his sleeping pattern. He must re-navigate his trek to find his original course or simply change headings altogether. He has to conceal his food source with much more diligence now as a result of his ordeal to keep other predators from seeking it and finding his location. Similarly, we were impacted as a generation during these troubling times of the 1960s. It was in fact like a ferocious beast attack on a generation.

Movies like *In the Heat of the Night* and *Guess Who's Coming to Dinner,* underscored the racial tension of the times through drama. We still produce war movies depicting the horror of Vietnam. What messages do youth receive today which shapes their character and self-images? I'm simply relating some relevant circumstances that were happening during the baby boomer's formative years and the resulting product it fashioned. From my example, we can more readily foresee some possibilities that may come about as a result of the type of world that we create for today's youth. Let's examine more 1960s realities that helped shape today's over 40's and 50's culture.

Also in 1968, what is known as the Orangeburg Massacre took place in Orangeburg, South Carolina. The shootings occurred on February 18th, two nights after students from an almost all-black college tried to bowl at the city's only bowling alley and were refused by the owner. Tensions rose and violence erupted. When it ended, nine students and one city policeman received hospital treatment for injuries. Other students were treated at the college hospital. College faculty and administrators at the scene witnessed at least two instances where female students were held by one officer and clubbed by others. In total, 28 students were injured and three lay dying.

As students began returning to the front to watch their bonfire go out, a patrolman suddenly squeezed off several rounds from his weapon into the air, reportedly intending them to be warning shots. As other officers began firing, students fled in panic or dived for cover. Many were shot in their backs and sides, and even the soles of their feet. Some warning shot!

The Kent State shootings, also known as the May 4th Massacre or Kent State Massacre, occurred at Kent State University in the city of Kent, Ohio. This incident involved the shooting of unarmed college students by members of the Ohio National Guard on Monday, May 4th, 1970. This took place at a time when I was an early teen, and during a time when my brother was preparing to become a student at Kent State University. We lived only 20 minutes from the scene of this tragedy. This tragic event had special significance to me personally and helped form opinions about the world. The guardsmen fired 67 rounds over a period of 13 seconds, killing four students and wounding nine others, one of whom suffered permanent paralysis.

I experienced the horror of being caught up in a riot that was happening as a result of the shooting of Nobel Peace Prize winner Dr. Martin Luther King, Jr. on April 4th, 1968. I and my siblings were returning home from vacation Bible School with one of the neighbors when we made a right turn on the wrong street and ran smack dab into the middle of the rioting. Bricks were thrown into the windshields of cars, buildings burning, windows broken, and I'll never forget the look of terror on the face of the man in the car which had just driven through the carnage.

He was driving South as we were going North on Edgewood street. Flushed red was his face as he had his head ducked down near the steering wheel to avoid being attacked by other rioters. He looked at us in our car as we passed each other. He was completely overcome with dread, terror and obvious alarm. He and I made brief eye contact; it was as if time moved in super slow motion, one frame at a time. I could see several bricks lodged in his front windshield. Damage on the front left fender and hood of the car. I believe that there were other people in the car with him but down on the floor, and in that millisecond that our eyes met he communicated his terror to me. I felt his consternation, which compounded my own fear. I felt his family's distress and had empathy with them. Then abruptly with the same suddenness as it slowed, time moved back to normal again, just like in the movies. A resident, an elderly African American woman, suddenly ran out to the road where we were traveling shouting *"**GO BACK! GO BACK, PLEASE GO BACK!**"* as she motioned us to turn around! Our driver, the neighbor from across the street put the car into reverse and speedily turned it around and fled in the other direction. There was a madness happening in our nation; we melted down to the lowest common denominator.

"You don't have to teach people how to be human. You have to teach them how to stop being inhuman." – Eldridge Cleaver

Eldridge Cleaver, whose most recognized book, *Soul on Ice,* was a prominent member of the Black Panther Party. During these times the Panther Party was at its most active. **Black Power** became the essence of a culture within a culture, often sparking clashes between the blacks and police. *"Say it loud, I'm black and I'm proud"* was in style. The rebellion was fully joined. On October 16th, 1968, an action by two so-called African-American sprinters at the Mexico City Olympics shook the sporting world, and our nation again. Tommie Smith and John Carlos, the gold and bronze medalists in the men's 200 meter race, took their places on the podium for the medal ceremony barefooted and wearing civil rights badges, they bowed down their heads and each raised a black-gloved fist as the Star Spangled Banner was played. Both of them were members of the Olympic Project for Human Rights.

In an immediate response to their actions, Smith and Carlos were suspended from the U.S. team and banned from the Olympic Village. Those who opposed the protest said the actions disgraced all Americans. Supporters, on the other hand, praised the men for their courage. As a young black person, it was very difficult for me to understand why these individuals were discharged from the team for silently demonstrating on a world stage the injustices they themselves and their fellows were facing on a daily basis at home in the United States. The whole silencing of Smith and Carlos reminded me more of the statement I heard at home regarding our family secrets *(and you better not tell nobody.)* America, like my father, didn't want anyone else to know that they were abusers! Why do oppressors have a need for the oppressed to remain silent, not to scream or tell someone else about the pain being inflicted upon them? Pain will make you yell out loud, or in the case of Smith and Carlos, silently demonstrate publicly!

In Chicago in this same infamous year of 1968, protestors came out to demonstrate against "the system" and demand an end to the Vietnam War. Only a few thousand people participated in the demonstrations; most of those were local, or had come to support their favorite Democratic candidates. Overwhelmingly outnumbered by law enforcement by five-to-one, the protestors demonstrated. Ultimately, by the end of the demonstration 589 people would be arrested and many more injured. Most of the hostility took place in the park when the police tried to enforce evening curfews. A legal rally in Grant Park ended when the police clubbed a teenager who was lowering an American flag while others tried to protect him.

Mayor Richard J. Daley requested and received 7,500 members of the Illinois National Guard to reinforce the 12,000 police officers. While the nominating speeches were being given at the amphitheater several miles away, outside people were pushed through plate glass windows when caught between guardsmen and police as they dispersed the crowd. TV cameras caught the terrible brutality of the authorities that day and the world watched. *"The whole world was watching,"* a reporter said later as he described the incident as a *"police riot"* which did more damage to Chicago's reputation and the chances of the Democratic Party than anything the protestors could have done.

With the women's liberation movement happening at the same time, it was very difficult to maintain one's equilibrium. If you paid enough attention to all that was unfolding before your very eyes it would make you dizzy. As Tom Brokaw put it, *"For many watching the women's movement unfold on their television screens, it seemed as if the entire social fabric of the nation was unraveling with frightening speed."*

I gained an understanding about our society during those times, yet never fully apprehending the foundational premise of what I understood. Conversely, the most insightful realization I achieved was that one cannot understand people by means of intellect and carnal wisdom alone; people were then and continue to be ensnared in a spiritual mêlée. According to the Manual, *"The weapons of our warfare are not carnal but mighty through God to the pulling down of these strongholds."* (2 Corinthians 10:4) Each generation has baggage which must be unpacked and stored neatly away. However, it seems that our unpacked baggage has passed down to the next generation.

Dr. Benjamin Spock,[3] a prominent voice of that era is credited with the following quotes (Source: Brainyquotes.com):

"I'm not a pacifist. I was very much for the war against Hitler and I also supported the intervention in Korea, but in this war we went in there to steal Vietnam."

"In our country today, very few children are raised to believe that their principal destiny is to serve their family, their country, or God."

As I stated earlier, due to my interpretation of the voices and images of my youth, certain inaccuracies in judgment were made. Some baggage takes a long time to unpack!

I began to realize that conflicting principles were contending for my dependence on the truths embedded within them. Some life experiences simply by the nature of the events themselves cause you to question the world as it exists, and one wonders if this is all there is or was meant to be. Moreover, one begins to speculate as to what can be done to make for a better, safer, more equitable or evenhanded society in which to bring up our young. I do not wish that my children would have to struggle with the same forces that I wrestled with growing up. I would like to end certain hardships so that the next generation is free to take the next step instead of fighting the same foe as our generation fought. We need our youth to make the kind of strides toward wholeness that are necessary for liberty, fullness, and freedom!

As adults, we ourselves teach youth prejudice, we teach our youth greed, we teach our youth hatred, selfishness, dishonesty, and many other biases. These are not natural or inborn tendencies, and just as we teach such practices and beliefs we can and must dismantle them for the betterment of tomorrow's generations. The greater good being served must be viewed as a possible and realistic goal. I have included personal experiences such as these because it is the most effective way for me to illustrate the types of impairments that can result from the careless actions of others in a young person's maturational development.

The truth is the best gift I can bequeath to my family and community. I cannot convince someone of something I do not know or believe myself. If I am misguided, unless somewhere along the way I find clarity, I will purposely or inadvertently misguide others by way of example. My hurts and shortcomings would be transmitted to the detriment of the next generation.

What is necessary with immediacy is that we search out truth and righteousness and begin to reconstruct our fractured environment without delay. Perhaps I myself more than anyone else need to set sail with renewed vigor to dismantle the ills of past misfortunes and begin strengthening the framework of a better, more profitable future prospect for myself and those following behind me. Each of us can only begin with ourselves.

The miscalculations of the course that I set sail upon many years ago as a result of flawed self-perceptions and world views must be challenged and realigned based on updated, accurate information. The hindering hand of the enemy to one's life and the lives of our youth must of necessity be removed immediately. Only then will I be more suited to guide those coming after me.

Many of us who were but youths in the 1950s, 1960s and 1970s can recall that politically, times were taxing. Publicly as well as privately we struggled as the war in Vietnam rolled on year after agonizing year. Nam images steadily streaming through our black and white TV set as Walter Cronkite descried the horrible details of how many were killed this week. Images of big guns firing, Agent Orange strafing, images of the war, dead and disfigured soldiers, people being labeled draft dodgers because they disagreed with and refused to fight in what was considered by many an unjust war. Images of Vietnamese children being shot and blown up still haunt us today. The Vietnamese man who was shot in the head execution style, which played over and over on the news and other programs, and the war images pictured in *Life* magazine, all are components in the makeup of that generations psyche.

We were scared of the bomb due to McCarthyism,[4] which is defined as: The intense opposition, countering, fear and or suspicion of Communism, particularly in the United States during the 1950s. The mass pressure, harassment, and or blacklisting used to pressure people to follow popular political beliefs. The hysteria was brought on in large part by the 1954 Army vs. McCarthy hearings which were televised. For 36 days, the nation watched and developed its beliefs about certain world politics. We were so afraid of the Communist because of the constant barrage of anti-Communist propaganda and Americanism hoopla. Some of us can remember the disaster drills we had to perform in school regularly as grade school children.

Remember the alarm siren would sound and we were hurried into the halls and instructed to stand against the lockers? We had to place our hands behind our heads with fingers inter-locked or had to crouch under our desks with our hands over the back of our head and neck. This was to supposedly protect us from the atomic blast that everyone was so sure that the Russians would level our cities with any day. Bomb shelters were in vogue and it was so necessary to have one because we were scared out of our wits by our own government and media.

We were fearful, similar to today with the terrorism threat levels going from red to yellow to green and then back again.

Oh, did I say that our government wants to keep us frightened? That must have been a slip of the tongue; I couldn't have meant to say anything like our own government wants its citizens afraid.

SideBar: *Well, all I can say about that is, the bully on the playground could only take the milk money from the other kids as long as they were all scared of him. When the scared kids joined together and stood up to the bully, he couldn't get the milk money anymore, Interesting analogy, Huh?*

Chapter Six

Be Not Afraid

As a young person, I was fortunate enough to witness the career of the great Muhammad Ali. As I stated earlier, he was one of my favorite heroes for many reasons. Ali was an individual who refused to allow others to contaminate or neutralize his resolve to reach his goal. He was born Cassius Marcellus Clay, Jr. on January 17, 1942. He is the only three-time World Heavyweight Champion, who is widely considered to be, if not the greatest, then certainly one of the greatest heavyweight championship boxers of all time.

As an amateur Clay won a gold medal in the light heavyweight division at the 1960 Summer Olympics in Rome. He changed his name to Muhammad Ali after joining the Nation of Islam in 1964, subsequently converting to the Sunni Islam faith in 1975. In 1967 Ali refused to be inducted into the U.S. military based on his religious beliefs and opposition to the Vietnam War. He was arrested and found guilty on draft evasion charges, stripped of his boxing title, and his boxing license was suspended. He was not imprisoned, but did not fight again for over three years while his appeal worked its way up to the U.S. Supreme Court. He was subsequently reinstated.

Nicknamed "The Greatest," Ali was involved in several historic boxing matches. My personal favorite was the trilogy of pugilistic matches he fought with his greatest rival, Joe Frazier. But the fight with the superman George Foreman was, in my opinion, a victory that set Ali apart as the most outstanding heavyweight fighter I have ever seen. Ali beat Foreman in an amazing boxing contest which featured brawn vs. brain, skill, and fortitude. He suffered only five losses with no draws in his career, amassing an astounding 56 wins, (37 knockouts and 19 decisions). While a young person, Clay was reported to have been very outgoing, as we know him to be. He decided that he would become the greatest boxer in the world when he was just 16 or 17 years old.

For standing by his personal and religious convictions and beliefs, he was not only ridiculed but in many cases deeply resented by some segments of society. I believe that the fact that Ali spoke forcefully and firmly about such beliefs added fuel to the fire of those who resented him. However, he did not relent or show any indication that he would concede to the pressure. Faith and a principled life will not always insure popularity with men, but will get the attention of God. Ultimately men will stand to recognize in a principled person a quality which could not be ignored or denied as somehow extraordinary. Most people are too afraid to stand up for what they believe. Truly, most have a fear of believing in something that would promote action. Most feel more comfortable fitting in with the status-quo masses. Ali accomplished great exploits and honors both during and after his boxing career. His accomplishments include, but are not limited to, the following:

1959: National Golden Gloves Light Heavyweight Champion.
1959: National Amateur Athletic Union champion.
1960: National Golden Gloves Light Heavyweight Champion.
1960: National Amateur Athletic Union champion.
1960: Gold medal, Rome Olympics, light-heavyweight boxing.
1964-67: World Heavyweight Champion.
1970: Dr. Martin Luther King Memorial Award.
1974: Sportsman of the Year.
1974: Fighter of the Year, Boxing Writers Association
1974-78: World Heavyweight Champion.
1978-79: World Heavyweight Champion.
1979: Honorary Doctorate of Humane Letters, Texas Southern University.
1979 Street named after him in Louisville, Kentucky.

1985: Recognized for long, meritorious service, World Boxing Association.
1987: Elected to Boxing Hall of Fame
1990: Inducted into International Boxing Hall of Fame.
1996: Lights Olympic torch, Atlanta.
1997: Arthur Ashe Award for Courage, ESPN.
1997: Essence Living Legend Award.

Is Ali an aberration, a peculiarity, a deviation from the norm? I included him as an example of how one individual's tremendous struggles were overcome, and question myself as to why so many of us shrink under much less pressure. Were accomplishments such as his not to be expected from individuals who are considered average or ordinary? Is it not true that faith in God and in yourself will propel you to become what you aspired to become?

By maintaining the integrity of your belief that God can transform a life into its desired intent, great things can be achieved? Why do the vast majority fail to realize their intrinsic potential? Why do but a mere few become self-actualized? A young person today can become one the greatest of tomorrow if proper methods are employed and maintained over the course of the life span.

Boxer, the great heavyweight champion George Foreman, has impressed me perhaps more than any other with his ability to stay with it. "Big George" came from a past filled with crime, poverty, trouble in school, and overcame many adversities to become one of the most prolific businessmen worldwide. Big George won the heavyweight championship for the second time at the age of 45, becoming the oldest individual to do so. He overcame crime, nicotine and alcohol addiction, while he honed his craft as a youth. While consumed with anger and self-doubt, Big George found inner strength that would later become dominating factors in his struggle to become "somebody." In my opinion, Mr. Forman has become successful because of a deep-rooted search for God in himself. As the Manual says, if we seek Him with our whole heart we will find Him. God is success personified; if we seek after Him, the closer we get to Him the closer we are to success.

We must affirm that God loves us and desires what is best for us. He has a purpose and a plan for the life He created in us. Fear has no place in the heart of an individual, and any adult who purposely or inadvertently instills fear in a young person's heart does a great disservice to that child and to all of humanity as well. To deprive a youth of the fullest opportunity to reach his or her greatest potential is to deprive all of humanity of greater outcomes, and I believe to do so is truly evil. During my own "comeupins" I internalized much of the world's ills, allowing them to shape attitudes in me, many of which were not beneficial. The Bible consistently reminds us to "fear not" and to be courageous. Boldness is expected of us as the soldiers that we are, whether we realize it or not! We are not to shrink from the enemy's boastings. Like King David when he was just a lad, he charged the giant Goliath fearlessly in full confidence that the God of Israel was with him and would surely see him to victory. David was subsequently called a man after God's own heart and rose to greatness. As in Ali's life, he refused to cave in to the pressures placed on him by the boxing commission, the government, and many others in society, and to date he is still called "the greatest."

Special Note: Young man, young lady, God has not given you a spirit of fear, but that of love, peace, and sound mind. Anything that challenges that truth is not of God and in time is destined to fail. Whether it is a world political stance, a home life situation, or a social or educational difficulty, don't cave in to it! Whether in wealth or poverty, hold on courageously and know that God is with you and that He has a reward for those that diligently seek

Him. So, seek Him early and often. Mother, father, teacher, or coach, anyone who has the charge of mentoring youthful hearts and minds, strengthen your resolve to leave a legacy of truth and courage for the generations coming behind you. God's Manual says that to whom much is given, much is required. It is indeed much to impart into someone else, certainly impacting the future of the human race is huge, therefore meditate on the importance of that young person in your life. They are like arrows in your quiver marked to hit the target you aim them to reach. The lives we live are like a range locator for the young life in our care. We select velocity, direction, and trajectory merely by the fact of our influence, whether positive or negative.

Many of today's youth may inwardly recognize or may feel that they could have missed developmental steps and aren't as fast-paced in areas of traditional education, moral or ethical wellbeing, as possibly they otherwise could be. Just like me in the example of my football coach pointing to my thin neck in a derogatory manner, calling for me to change something I had no idea of how to change, and I thus quit the team. I opted out; just gave up in large part I believe because I had no blueprint for successfully altering what was presently demanded.

Have large portions of the younger generation decided to quit on us? Do we ridicule, speak harmful, destructive, and damaging words to our young, which over time may become injurious to their wellbeing? Remembering that life and death is in the power of the tongue, we must take care to select our words wisely. We have the power to either bless or curse with our mouths. Can there be some presumptions that can be understood in the distancing of youth from today's mainstream ideology in the question just posed? I suppose there have been generational gaps since time and families were founded. I would further venture to guess that the gradation to which we see gaps today is startling and unprecedented.

Showing signs of weakness or being soft is not permitted nowadays, so one must put on a hard exterior. Kids become hard because they believe that's its necessary to survive, while inside quietly suffering the pain of their reality. Inside it hurts that mom and dad fight all the time or are not involved in their lives. Wanting to be like a neighbor or the image on TV but not knowing how, or not having resources to purchase the advertised items their friends seem to have hurts deep inside but it can't be shown.

The Manual says, *"For as a man thinks in his heart, so is he."* (Proverbs 23:7) Subconsciously, I think I'm tough, therefore I am. I think I must be a brick wall so I am. If no one is going to be there to help me address my issues then I must convince myself that they don't exist in my world. From the vantage point as a young person it may appear that mom and dad are very busy building and maintaining their status of living, or the lack of any semblance to a standard. They are so into the church and each other or other outside activities. It may seem that dad is so into sports with his buddies or tired from work that I must make it pretty much on my own when it comes to life decisions and lifestyle choices. However, when I make a mistake only then do I get their full attention. They tell me what I did was stupid. I hear the message that I will grow up to become a nothing or either I get the crap beat out of me. How about helping me, guiding me before I make the mistakes? Even if I act like I know it all already, inside you and I both know I need you and I long for you more than anything. And if I make a mistake help me to truly learn from it without wounding me further. My blunders already hurt badly enough. So, let's be real with each other and come to an understanding, can you dig it?

Sidebar: *Cause and effect is real; if I don't change my baby's dirty diaper and he begins to smell badly how can I accuse him of stinking? If he eats he's going to poop and some foods make* *poop smell worse than others. What's my child eating? Who feeds him? Is it altogether his fault that his poop smells badly? Diets consist not only of food but words and actions. Is my child feeding on a diet of love, positive reinforcement and affirmation, or is it more of put-downs, negative reinforcements, haunts and hurts? The only thing that can come out is what has gone in. Let's truly ponder that point for a moment. Who feeds your child and what does his or her diet consist of?*

Has the adult population of today, who were the baby-boomers of yesterday, who in the 1950s and 1960s were themselves teens, let today's youth down instead of them letting us down? Is there a step in the spiritual maturational development of our youth missing due to key elements we have failed to impart? Or do we simply have a standoff with adults on one hand feeling that our youth are wayward without recourse, a lost generation? Or on the other hand could youth perhaps feel that today's adults do not or will not understand them or that adults care more about themselves and the activities they are preoccupied with? Could it be that we are busy in pursuing our pleasures, goals, and fantasies, and have in essence set our young to the side and don't really notice their pain?

Reaction to pain manifests itself in many ways. Could we be witnessing some of those manifestations in our youth today as we observe self-will, aggressiveness, highly active libidos, *"I don't care attitudes,"* disrespectfulness, and so on? If any of these questions can be answered *"Yes,"* or we are unsure, then what adjustments would need to be made and in whose lap does such fine-tuning of relations rest? I am not speaking to you about your kids only, but as a union of adults, how do we relate to our youth as a whole? Does the responsibility for life choices truly reside with the inexperienced or as an adult shall I demand more of myself as it relates to my child as well as the youth community at large?

The evidence that we as caregivers have, in essence, fumbled the ball, is irrefutable. But be not dismayed, we are not alone and it can be recovered. Generation upon generation before us has mishandled the transition from one age band to the next. We are now witnessing the blundering attempted handoff fall to the turf only to be recovered by the opposing team. There are few downs remaining and the clock is ticking. We must get a defensive stop and force the opposing team to punt. Once the ball is back in our possession we must then resolve to make a clean transfer of the ball into the hands of this generation who as the running back can gain yardage. With adequate play calling and skilled blocking they can score many touchdowns as they go forward to help humanity win the all-important championship ring.

I will conclusively demonstrate just how we have supported the failure of the next generation, and what we can and must do to foster greater hope and correct the errors that we have made as we go along from here. The truth is, all is not lost by any means, but great hope and tremendous possibilities still exist for us and our youth. If we can admit our shortcomings and resolve to courageously redirect our futures, great things can happen. Stand your ground in full assurance of God's great power to uphold you, as we do we will pave a brave new environment for our youth to grow, flourish, and build upon for themselves and generations to follow. Without fear or trepidation, with all due diligence, let us move from here with the knowledge that we can see significant and encouraging transformations if we are vigilant and courageous.

Chapter Seven

Responsible Leadership

Incorrigibility has been and remains something that societies must deal with in youth and adult populations alike. We must not or cannot shrink from that accountability as a civilization. To love, nurture, groom, guide, empower, correct and stand beside our youth for their greater good is fundamental and vital for the wellbeing of any group or society. This is an indispensable truth that every civilization or family must come to terms with if it is to survive.

We would do very well to see to the welfare of our young from a perspective that we are not in and of ourselves the ultimate authority on living our lives. There is a loftier perch from which we can gain a better comprehension of what life is and what it can be. We must fully understand where we are along the human experience continuum.

Sidebar: *If I live to be 155 years old, I will have seen much and developed a wide view of Earthly realties. However, if I received the "wisdom of the ages" from an all-knowing being who existed from the beginning of time; someone who spanned into the outer reaches of eternity, I then would be able to share much more with those who come behind me? Would I not then be in a better position to understand myself and those around me?*

I observed the power of peer pressure while teaching in the classroom setting. There were kids I knew that wanted to learn what I was there to teach. Small clusters of youths would sit together in what appeared to be cells of restrained desire, wanting to demonstrate how smart they were and that they wanted better for themselves now and in the future. I could tell that they were inhibited by peer pressure to freely express this. They simply wanted the acceptance of the "hip" crowd. Oh sorry, hip is not hip to say any more. What I mean to say is they wanted to be "down witit" too.

Sidebar: "Down witit" is a very interesting variation of terms. It's a colloquial manner of saying "to be with it." It is pronounced witit. In a manner of speaking, wit is an alternative way of saying intelligence, understanding, or sharpness. Contrastingly, to be "down witted" seems to indicate lower intelligence, understanding, or sharpness. I don't think I would feel comfortable using the term in this way.

I couldn't help gravitating to these young people, more than once I asked them to come to the front of the room, away from all the distractions, where I could provide a more uninterrupted lesson. These groups were not considered to be the cool kids or trendy groups. They were very nice, well-mannered, and obviously well taught at home. They simply did not want to be disliked by the larger, more unrestrained, disinterested group. They wanted to fit in, and they wanted to follow the leaders. How do we factor leadership into our social relations? Does it matter to the rest of the body what decisions are made by the head of that body? As the heads of our households and communities, is what we do impacting our youth in any way? Have you ever wondered why the coach gets fired when a team is doing poorly?

A team takes on the persona or attitude of the coach. A coach leads the team to a perceived goal by developing a mindset in the team, and focuses the team in one direction. Also, coaches build secondary strengths which support the primary purpose, which is to win games. Some secondary supports could include body strengthening, endurance, unity, and education with regard to the sport the team plays, and isolation of the team within reason. By isolation I mean keeping the members of the team clear from negative attitudes and perceptions that would hinder its primary goal – which is to win!

The same is true about the corporate world. Managers, Executive Directors and CEO's and their staff develop the team concept for the business or any other successful organization. Whatever the purpose of the company or organization, the head is largely responsible to develop and lead the team.

Think about church leadership for a moment. When the congregation is growing and the community is engaged in what the local church is doing, people becoming converted and church donations increase. Consequently, new land may be purchased and new construction may begin. Also, community programs may expand and go forward. Then, what do people say? *"Pastor so-and-so is doing great things."* By contrast, if a church is perceived to be failing, and donations are down and the congregation is scattering we say, *"Something must be wrong with the pastor or his or her ministry, and the board of directors may seek to replace him or her or find creative ways to refocus."*

Uniformly when it comes to parenting, this dynamic can also be seen. Surely you have heard similar statements as these: *"Judging by the way Allen and Belinda turned out I can tell that their parents did a good job with them."* Or conversely *that, "Terrance is always in trouble; what's the problem, where are his parents?"* Or the example I gave about my friend and his family in a previous chapter wherein I stated that his children were doing well because of him and his wife and the love and care they provide is a perfect case in point. I attributed the success of his children to him and his wife. I am sure you know of instances where you could plug in so many other names among those you personally are acquainted with who have children who are doing very well and some who are doing very poorly. In these cases, you most likely would assign praise or blame to the parent.

At this point I believe I have laid sufficient groundwork and have a firm basis to make the following assertions: In our world and in our homes as the parents go, so goes the child and family. Likewise, as our societal, political, religious and business leaders go, so goes our nation and world.

The next paragraph is inserted from an email I received from a friend:

Accounts Receivable Tax, Building Permit Tax, CDL License Tax, Cigarette Tax, Corporate Income Tax, Dog License Tax, Federal Income Tax, Federal Unemployment Tax, Fishing License Tax, Food License Tax, Fuel Permit Tax, Gasoline Tax, Hunting License Tax, Inheritance Tax, Inventory Tax, IRS Interest Charges (tax on top of tax), IRS Penalties (tax on top of tax), Liquor Tax, Luxury Tax, Marriage License Tax, Medicare Tax, Property Tax, Real Estate Tax, Service charge taxes, Social Security Tax, Road Usage Tax (Truckers) Sales Taxes, Recreational Vehicle Tax, School Tax, State Income Tax, State Unemployment Tax (SUTA), Telephone Federal Excise Tax, Telephone Federal Universal Service Fee Tax, Telephone Federal, State and Local Surcharge Tax, Telephone Minimum Usage Surcharge Tax, Telephone Recurring and Non-recurring Charges Tax, Telephone State and Local Tax, Telephone Usage Charge Tax, Utility Tax, Vehicle License Registration Tax, Vehicle Sales Tax, Watercraft Registration Tax, Well Permit Tax, and Workers Compensation Tax. Not one of these taxes existed 100 years ago...and our nation was the most prosperous in the world. We had absolutely no national debt... We had the largest middle class in the world... and mom stayed home to raise the kids.

Now mom works just like dad — if there is a dad in the home at all. The family has been under attack for years and its foundations are weakening under the strain. We are redefining marriage and family. The home is the base point and spring-board from which societies are spawned. If home is functioning well then it follows reason that a higher probability for successful community life will result.

Leadership begins at home as we model lifestyle profiles for our youth. Teachers and clergy are also early role models for youth. Young people take prompts from their friend's parents as they visit and view how things are handled in different house-holds also, comparing what is acceptable there versus in their own home.

Sports and other media figures, while only human and prone to making mistakes, grow to be looked upon as iconic trail-blazers who many youths attempt to emulate as well. Political dignitaries and money moguls who make the decisions that steer our lives are also watched closely, bringing our attention to bear on what they do as they plot the course of our nation and our lives.

The typical worldview of a person in their early post teen years promotes self-centeredness; the right to happiness and self-fulfillment is at the center of these attitudes. The impor-tance of personal expression in all forms are displayed. They seem to easily tolerate aberrant or immoral points of views, allowing for disrespect of other people. Use of profanity and the advance of all forms of generic spirituality that dismiss the validity of the Judeo-Christian faith seem to be at the core.

In many of today's youth we find that the *"I don't give a f--k"* attitude runs amuck whether it is spoken or expressed through body language or other ways. Largely propelled by postmodern thought, the typical worldview of many young people does not facilitate respect for life, acceptance of the rule of law, or the necessity of hard work or personal sacrifice. Doing what is necessary to make a better community doesn't seem to have any place in this mind set. Paying one's dues or contributing to the common good are somehow absent. Also, only about 2% of today's teenagers possess a working biblical view that acknowledges the existence of God, Satan, and sin, according to some reports. It's sort of "anything goes." Everything is subjective to ones likes or dislikes; if it's good to you then it's alright. The availability of forgiveness and grace through Christ, and the existence of absolute moral principles provided in the Bible don't seem to factor into this mentality. Sadly, overall Christian teens don't fare much better than secular ones.

Modest estimates from conservative denominations show that 70% of children from Christian households are "toying with the faith!" They are saving it until they have had their so-called fun.

I believe that if this is true, it's true because of lifestyles prior generations have modeled for today's youth. We have men and women cohabitating without the sacred bond of marriage, raising children who have no concept or reference of what marriage truly, authentically, and realistically is. We demonstrate by example men with men and women with women raising children in homes as being "normal." Moreover, in some states these same types of relationships are provided with the same endorsement by law as marriage between one man and one woman.

Traditional marriage between one man and one woman may seem foreign to the youths growing up in such an "alternative" home environment. Subsequently the impact of peer pressure upon a youth from such a home upbringing could foster further breaks from conventional standards. The perceptions and beliefs held by youth from such homes in defense and support of their loved ones utilizing peer pressure tend to intimidate other youth from traditional backgrounds and beliefs, thus fostering an acceptance of the encroaching alternative lifestyles.

Tiger and Elin Woods, and so many others who are in the public eye, suffered stress in their marriage as just about any marriage does. Instead of honoring vows made on the wedding day, they destroy the union. This brings one question to mind: *"What's love got to do with it?"* It seems that people get married nowadays with the expectation that it will end and when it's over our spouse feels that they should be somehow compensated or enriched for services rendered. The very person we entered into covenant with, we now must "take to the cleaners for all we can get," seems to be the mindset: We must hurt them as much as possible, or at the very least be as heartless as we can be. Is that a good thing to teach our youth?

Many times, the youths birthed from the union between feuding couples are the very weapons used against the other spouse. Is there any love or forgiveness in the world today? Is there any remorse or repentance left in anyone's heart today?

If one partner repents, does the one-time best friend and life companion have to be so compelled to avenge themselves that they must also renege on the promise they also made to their partner in front of the entire wedding guest list? We also break our promise to the pastor who married us, and to God who joined us together, as well as the promise we make to ourselves. While all in attendance at the wedding witnessed the happy couple being whisked away to honeymoon bliss and life happily ever after, now some of the same individuals give witness at divorce proceedings. When we say, *"I do,"* what real value does that have? Is it just a formality of the ceremony that really has no significance anymore?

The prenuptial agreement signifies an expectation of an impending fatality of a marriage before it even begins. Why get married and make vows to love, cherish, and keep one's self reserved only to your spouse in sickness and health, for richer or poorer, till death do you part, if divorce is around the corner? We proudly declare these promises in the presence of God and all in attendance on our most special day, simply to forfeit when we decide that sexual infidelity with someone else will suit us better.

We say with our mouth that we are married, but our hearts and minds remain single. We look only for what we can gain but seldom look for what we can give. We convince ourselves that if my spouse has gained weight or maybe the money is not right, I have the right to have sex with someone who is more attractive now. Or a co-worker makes me laugh and they really understand me so it's OK to flirt, knowing full well that flirting can lead down the primrose path to intimacy. Already having fantasized about becoming romantically involved, yet continuing to allow temptation to beckon. Or we pursue the old girlfriend that has always been there for us; the one woman who had the string to our heart and knew exactly how to pull it. We allow such a one to become the center of our affectionate attention even though we have a spouse to whom we have given our most sincere promise. She was the one girl you refused to separate yourself from completely once you were married. She was the one that, from time to time, you called on the phone just to say *"Hello!"* You knew in your heart of hearts you were rolling the dice each time you called, and hoping that one day they would turn up in your favor. We disavow our oath for temporary gratification. As a society, we have unequivocally lost our doggone minds!

Yes, we have lost something as a culture; it appears that common sense can be found arguably, only in history books nowadays. Whoever goes before another by that fact is the leader. Leadership of our youth comes from us, and we are setting a shameful and dangerous precedence in full view of those we mislead through the undefined present into the shadowy future.

Let's ask ourselves what happened to real love and commitment, and how does the shocking divorce statistics speak to our youth?

At DivorceStatistics.info it has been reported *that "Various studies on US rate of divorce show significant differences when a comparison is made in 1st, 2nd and 3rd marriage breakups in America."* For example, in America for first marriages the divorce rate is from 41- to 50%. The divorce rate for second marriage jumps to 60- to 67%. Lastly, divorce rates for third marriage ranges from an astounding 73- to 74%. Couples with children reportedly have a slightly lower rate of divorce as compared to couples with no children. Tragically, children of divorced parents are four times more likely to divorce than children of parents who remain together.

Our kids are watching, learning, and growing. Look at what we are showing them; as leaders look at where we are leading them. Understanding that the path upon which we lead them is the same pathway that they will lead their children on, even as our parents led us. What is the expected outcome of all of this? Will family be elevated or debased? When our youth and theirs after them continue this trend, will there be anything left that resembles a family in 40 years?

In First Corinthians, Chapter Seven, Paul tells us the following: *"Nevertheless, to avoid fornication, let every man have his own wife, and let every woman have her own husband. Let the husband render unto the wife due benevolence: and likewise also the wife unto the husband. The wife hath not power of her own body, but the husband: and likewise also the husband hath not power of his own body, but the wife. Defraud ye not one the other, except it be with consent for a time, that ye may give yourselves to fasting and prayer; and come together again, that Satan tempt you not for your inability. But I speak this by permission, and not of commandment. For I wish that all men were even as I myself. But every man hath his proper gift of God, one after this manner, and another after that. I say therefore to the unmarried and widows, it is good for them if they abide even as I. But if they cannot contain, let them marry: for it is better to marry than to burn.*

"And unto the married I command, yet not I but the Lord: Let not the wife depart from her husband. But and if she does depart, let her remain unmarried or be reconciled to her husband: and let not the husband put away his wife. But to the rest speak I, not the Lord: If any brother hath a wife that believeth not, and she is pleased to dwell with him, let him not put her away. And the woman who hath a husband that believeth not, and if he be pleased to dwell with her, let her not leave him. For the unbelieving husband is sanctified by the wife, and the unbelieving wife is sanctified by the husband: else were your children unclean; but now are they holy. But if the unbelieving depart, let him depart. A brother or a sister is not under bondage in such cases: but God hath called us to peace."

And again, in the Holy Bible's Book of Ephesians, Chapter Five, we are instructed as follows: *"Giving thanks always for all things unto God and the Father in the name of our Lord Jesus Christ; submitting yourselves one to another in the fear of God. Wives, submit yourselves unto your own husbands, as unto the Lord. For the husband is the head of the wife, even as Christ is the head of the church: and he is the messiah of the body. Therefore as the church is subject unto Christ, so let the wives be to their own husbands in everything. Husbands, love your wives, even as Christ also loved the church, and gave himself for it; That he might sanctify and cleanse it with the washing of water by the word, That he might present it to himself a glorious church, not having spot, or wrinkle, or any such thing; but that it should be holy and without blemish. So ought men to love their wives as their own bodies. He that loves his wife loves himself. For no man ever yet hated his own flesh; but nourishes and cherishes it, even as the Lord the church: For we are members of his body, of his flesh, and of his bones. For this cause shall a man leave his father and mother, and shall be joined unto his wife, and the two shall be one flesh."*

We see far too many instances of wives submitting to men other than their own husbands and too many husbands giving themselves to wives who are not their own. And we have the unmarried submitting to fornication with whomever they please without any conscience of wrong doing whatsoever. Sadly, those of us who confess religious beliefs, do not fare much better than those who have no such confession of faith in these matters. Is this the best lesson we can teach to our youth and future generations? The corner toward selfishness and "me, myself, and I," has been turned. If we could put just one generation of true God seekers out on the playing field, individuals who seek God's will and not our own will, we would see the world for many thousands of generations to come change for the better.

As stated previously, we have come apart at the seams and must employ a holistic approach toward recovery if any verifiable upsurge is to be achieved. Spiritually, religiously, educationally, politically, socially, economically, we must find a way to renovate ourselves. There must be real transformation and our youth must receive our love and redirection as well. As a society, we can and must provide this blueprint for transformation to our youth without fail for the betterment of all humanity. Family values and moral ascent were the norm for the most part in communities as we came along as younglings. For the most part, our fore-parents cared about right and wrong. We made the decisions to turn our attention to other less commendable pursuits with the recompense rightfully being ours. We should not pass this heritage on to our children and their offspring after them.

Sidebar: *If I stole an apple from the fruit stand, I should make restitution before I'm jailed and not leave my son or yours to bare the consequence of my wrongdoing. I should not leave his ability to purchase at the same fruit stand tarnished. I should not handcuff him with my errors, but leave him free, if not in better standing. As a leader, I must keep the path free of my debris knowing there are those who follow.*

Let's look at some of the other ways in which we have rent the fabric of the authentic while endeavoring to repair that fabric with artificial thread. Let's look at these in order that we may know where we went amiss and make healthy strides to realign ourselves with truth. It's incredible how so many of us become Pharisees and Sadducees and lose sight of ourselves as such. Readily we point out the splinter in another eye, failing to realize that we have a huge log in our own. Many of us place self-righteousness above Christ's true righteousness! I'm no judge or jury in this matter; just ringing the alarm bell.

Chapter Eight

Politics and Business Leaders

I believe it is imperative that we adults see ourselves in the light of truth and make the necessary amendments to our own lives first, then the lives of our youth can follow.

We have our mayors, governors, representatives, senators, and sorry to say yes, our presidents and world leaders from every genre who openly lie, cheat, and steal without a smidgen of remorse. Remember Watergate? What about Bill Clinton's public declaration that *"I did not have sex with that woman!"* which was found to be an obvious lie? These are the lies we know about. Ordinary folk like you and me may never become fully aware of the real secrets and lies. These real undetected lies should be the ones of upper-most concern.

Political scandals, our business practices, the overwhelming assault of commercial advertising which promises big and delivers little, all make the quicksand of "trickeration" much deeper and harder to climb out of. Remember the AIG scandal? And what about Bernie Madoff who made-off with millions of dollars which he pilfered from investors? Have you noticed how products are packaged and sold nowadays?

Do you buy potato chips? Have you noticed how the top half of the bag is filled with air while only the bottom half contains a small quantity of chips? This model has become a standard metaphor for selling to the consumer these days. Give as little as you can get away with and charge as much as possible for it, all the while pitching, *"new and improved, everybody has this and you must have this too or else you're a nobody and life is passing you by."* Why do we continue to allow such practices to be employed at our expense?

"What luck for rulers that men do not think." — Adolf Hitler

In 1962 the U.S. Supreme Court ruled that prayer in America's public schools was unconstitutional when directed by a state government. In 1963 the Court ruled that it was unconstitutional for the state to sponsor Bible reading or the praying of the Lord's Prayer in public schools. In 1980 the U.S. Supreme Court ruled that it was unconstitutional for the Ten Commandments to be posted in a public school classroom. In 1992 the Court ruled that it was unconstitutional for the state to sponsor prayer at school promotional activities and graduation ceremonies. Lastly, in 2000 the U.S. Supreme Court ruled that student-led, student initiated prayer before a football game was unconstitutional.

Keep in mind that we are a nation built upon the premise, "In God we trust." We and our parents have allowed this basic tool of collective prayer in our schools to be taken from today's youth without protest. The platform they used to remove prayer from public places stated that organized prayer in schools was a violation of the principle of "separation of church and state." Clearly, we are experiencing the equivalent of sabotage of our nation and the moral crippling of future generations due in part to this indignity.

Most of us above the age of 40 or 50 may remember what school was like during the days in which we were allowed to pray and seek God's guidance at school. It was decided that publicly funded schools were an extension of the state, and that organized prayer or Bible readings were a form of proselytizing. The bans not only expelled mandatory prayer in schools but also prohibited the daily reading of Bible passages as well.

Corporately seeking God's wisdom, guidance, and aid side by side with one's cohorts is necessary to being truly successful in life. Not only in church do we need to seek God's wisdom, it must be a way of life for all mankind in every corner of this world. If indeed we trust in God then why would we eject His obviously much needed aid and guidance from our upcoming generations in their formative years?

The Manual says if a man desires to be successful, let him pray. It follows reason then, if the family wants to be successful, let its members pray. If the class or school wants their students to be successful, let them pray and ask of the one from whom success comes. If our cities, states, and nation want to be successful, let us corporately pray. You have not because you ask not! However, we forsook prayer to gain what?

Are we better off today now that we cannot pray in school? I think not. Contrast a typical classroom setting from 40 years ago with a typical classroom setting today. As illustrated from the outset of this book, the incidents of violence between students and against staff has spiked dramatically. Test scores are sliding with no breakwater in place to halt the slide. Look closely at our prison population comparatively with college graduation rates. There should be an overwhelmingly dramatic difference on the side of college students graduating and pursuing gainful careers to aid mankind. However, our prisons are filled to the point that they are overflowing, and we have new so-called correctional facilities being built all the time to imprison more individuals.

According to a periodical from the Bureau of Justice Statistics[1] posted September 2015, *"The United State held an estimated 1,561,500 prisoners in state and federal custody at the end of 2014."* This same article further states that *"Nearly 3% of non-Hispanic black males and 1% of Hispanic males were serving sentences of at least 1 year in prison at year-end 2014, compared to less than 0.5% of non-Hispanic white males. An estimated 516,900 black males (37%), 453,500 white males (32%), and 308,700 Hispanic males (22%) were in custody. Black men had the highest imprisonment rate in every age group and were in state or federal facilities 3.8 to 10.5 times more often than white men and 1.4 to 3.1 times more often than Hispanic men."*

The Washington Post[1] reported the following information on January 6, 2015: *"To put these figures in context, we have slightly more jails and prisons in the U.S. — 5,000 plus — than we do degree-granting colleges and universities. In many parts of America, particularly the South, there are more people living in prisons than on college campuses."*

Removing God and prayer from our public schools seems to have eliminated ingredients in the stew of community health that should not have continued unchallenged!

The lawsuits over prayer in public schools were supported by several organizations, but the most outspoken supporter for banning prayer in schools came from Madelyn Murray O'Hair, the founder of American Atheists, Inc. The world is made up of leaders and followers, and the Manual repeatedly referred to the masses as sheep that need a Sheppard. We must wisely decide which voice we will follow. Those who desire the best for our nation and its future generations remained conspicuously silent while this essential component to human existence was summarily stripped away.

School is a vitally important place we send our young to be educated, second only to the home. Genuine education cannot take place in the absence of ultimate truth being present and communicated. How long will we remain silent onlookers while individuals with little or no valid understanding make the decisions that impact the future of our nation which adversely affect our grandchildren and their children after them? When will the voices of the silent majority be heard with sufficient intensity to cast off the burdensome yoke of the foolish?

As church parishioners, we more often than not conceal ourselves out of sight and out of earshot of the world. We huddle in relatively small clusters on Sunday mornings while those who demonstrate and march on Washington to shred the moral fabric of our nation and the world instill error into our cultural cloth. They make themselves heard on Capitol Hill while the voices of church leaders reach only as far as the back pew. From congregation to congregation the focus of the messages is so incongruent that no real headway or progress is ever even imagined as something to be desired. They march down Main Street making a lot of noise and gaining a lot of attention. We preach, shout, and give our monies at church and then go home only to blend into the fabric which is being woven by the unholy. We meet the next week at church again and have another good old time in secret away from the areas where the dismantling of righteousness is taking place. We somehow rationalize this as an acceptable lifestyle for the Christian. When will we rise to the call of shaping our world instead of being shaped by the world? It is my belief that we can and should be thermostats setting the temperature and not simply thermometers revealing the coldness of our commitment to what we claim to believe!

Jesus was criticized because he went out into the community and taught by demonstration that the Kingdom of God was at hand. He sat eating and drinking with those considered sinners. Jesus rubbed elbows with non-religious folk as well as religious. He was accused of eating with sinners and tax collectors and called a wine bibber by the Pharisees of his day. Many of us today might point the finger at him also while we stand refusing to get our own hands dirty with the un-churched or those wicked folks we love to talk about and hear about so much.

As leaders, we must lead with the knowledge that others are following as we show the way. We must voice our views in a public forum not once a year during black history month or special days like resurrection day or Christmas or perhaps some contrived holiday. We must, with equal or greater intensity and frequency, speak out as those who disdain godliness. If we stood up against the encroachment of wrongdoing, would not our youth consider it? Let's set examples of concern for what happens in our communities; examples that youth could grab hold of. It's not that one must always be pumping his fist in the air and shouting in the streets *"THE END IS NEAR; THE END IS NEAR!"* By contrast remaining silent while truth and righteousness is whittled away layer after layer is not acceptable either.

If we sit in front of our TV sets viewing the news in disgust with the crime, political corruption, religious improprieties, and depravity in the streets, and just shake our heads and move on to listen to the next story, what will we continue to get? More of the same! Another new and more shocking story of spiritual abandon is what we will continue to get. They line up like airplanes over the landing strip waiting to land on our minds and hearts, forcing us to back away from the belief that we are empowered to do anything about it. This too is a falsehood. There is strength in prayerful unity.

There is power in the representation of our common interests. But there is utter weakness in the fragmented, dismantled policy of separation as we sit, each in our homes, and cry *"Oh my, that's awful,"* yet doing nothing. Separation of Church and State is obviously a ploy by the enemy to weaken our strength and cause us to pause while evil runs unchecked. Our youth are not only learning to allow whatever evil coming down the pipe to flow unimpeded, but they lean from us that trying to halt or repel it is not an option. I say *"No"* to that. The words in the Manual clearly tell us to have no fellowship with the unfruitful works of darkness, but rather reprove them. To do nothing while evil surges forward is to condone it. Shadrach, Meshach, and Abednego refused to bend the knee and pay homage to what was contrary to their belief in God. Although thrown into the fire, they were exonerated; hence we still tell of their courage and resolve today.

Stay the course! Stay on track! Do not relent, but remain resolute and hopeful. Forty years after we're gone they will talk of our courage and determination. But more importantly they will benefit from our heroic stance. They will fondly recall how our contribution to humanity was the indispensable turning point at which mankind began to awaken.

The Workplace

We spend nearly one third of our lives at work or in work related activity. Therefore, of necessity, the workplace is another area that must be examined. Individuals who work the hardest make the least money in our culture's cast system, and seemingly every attempt is vigorously made to hold individuals at the level of income that the previous position provided. There seems to be some upward flexibility as we progress. However, more often than not wages appear to come down as companies seek out new and creative methods to cut costs. Nowadays it appears that reducing one's standard of living would be a more accurate assessment of what's happening.

Paradoxically the mantra, *"Work hard and believe in yourself, put your time in to make that money, keep your nose to the grindstone, trade time for dollars,"* is instilled in the youth of lower wage earners, but a very different way of thinking is implied for those who are the top income earners or the wealthy: *"It's not enough that I succeed, but my competitors must fail. Crush or amalgamate the competition; I don't work hard for money; money works hard for me. I work smarter not harder."* As the Borg of *Star Trek: The Next Generation* announces upon their arrival, *"You will be assimilated; resistance is futile,"* so marches the opulent.

Slavery in this country was first an economic system; it became more of a racially oppressive way of life as the economic system of slavery was threatened. It became more closely associated with what we know as slavery today when fear of lifestyle changes for the power structure elite became real.

It's interesting to me personally as I look at the chain of command in manufacturing plants and see how similar they are structured when compared to the old slave plantations. The newest employee receives the most difficult task and the least pay; work is scrutinized by a foreman or overseer who is set in place to keep the whip "a crackin." The foreman has more liberties and earning potential than the rank and file employee. The foreman is quite commonly an individual of non-colored descent. Above the foreman we have the department heads, managers, vice presidents, and presidents, again most commonly non-blacks. But the owner is free of the daily duties of running the plant and has the highest earning capacity. That's very similar to the way the old slave plantations operated! Hmmm! (Plant-plantation? Too similar!)

Real slavery is still practiced in some places under the name of Civilian Inmate Labor Program. It is a cost-effective program for the U.S. Army, which receives federal prisoners from the Federal Bureau of Prisons (FBOP). Under this program the U.S. Attorney General provides federal prisoners to other federal agencies, which decide the types of services the prisoners can and will perform.

When younger inner city job seekers look at how future challenges are very likely to play out with low paying tedious jobs, truths such as plantation politics as we discussed in the previous paragraph may cause some alarm and make such work undesirable. Remember, we have a generation of calculating, shrewd, and perceptive individuals following behind us. We have taught them very well that it's all about the money honey; the more you have the more you are, and the less you have the less you are. Many youths select educating themselves and seeking the better positions in the corporate sector. I hope that the trend towards education and technical knowledge grows faster than that of the downward drift. I believe it can.

Perhaps an equal amount of the potential workforce if not more, work in factory or service oriented jobs, or are unemployed altogether. Many involve themselves in various other occupations to get by. We have taught youth to get as much as they can as fast as they can; that your worth as a human being is directly fixed to what possessions and money you have. Other virtues seemingly mean next to nothing. With protocol being established, we provide such mindsets. Prior establishments have made this very clear.

Who, pray tell, is the establishment? We are! Government, business, religions, media, and sport organizations are all just groups of ordinary people; the adult population. We built upon the framework left to us by our predecessors. We comprise the whole of the established order. We built upon what our fathers left us and our fathers built upon what their fathers left them. Now it comes to the youth generation of today. Will the path of shame and nakedness continue to be constructed or will our youth choose a more excellent way? How can we help the next generation make more quality choices for their lives? Choices superior to the ones we have made!

When I was a young boy we had a saying regarding *"Movin on up."* It went like this: *"Good better best, never let it rest, till the good gets better and the better gets best!"* Quite applicable I would say! We always say that we want our kids to do better than we have done; we have the opportunity to teach them to do so. A current news report announced that for the first time since reconstruction our youth will not do as well as their parents. Let us give our youth every advantage by setting the proper examples and appropriate leadership. We can help bring about the realization of the hope we have for our youth by what we do today. I'm not speaking to the isolated pockets of parents and individuals who have fitting postures in the community only. That's not enough! We must show a united front if we are to address this growing cultural dilemma. Wrong anywhere is a dismantler of right everywhere. Our youth will never get a clear portrait if those who see inappropriate behavior do nothing about it just because they are not the one engaging in it. We must help our brothers and sisters see how we are all connected and every act impacts the next action. In the game of chess each move sets up the reaction of the opponent and subsequently your next move. Let your next move be your best move.

Take the Risk: Believe!

Do you now or have you ever smoked pot, used alcohol and or other drugs? What about smoking cigarettes or any form of drug use or risk-taking behavior? Morning caffeine fix maybe? Daily prescription medication uses perhaps, or sugar, gambling, sex, over-eating, possibly one of these things may be your bag. Alcohol abuse kills some 75,000 Americans each year. Those who give themselves to it while it is legal do a great disservice to themselves and their lineage.

We tend to overindulge ourselves with television, sports, the arts, education, and so many more pursuits. When I see today's youth using tobacco products, alcohol and other drugs, it is painful and disturbing.

While clearly drug use and abuse takes place in every sector of society, invariable law enforcement remains conspicuously encamped in poorer inner city neighborhoods to fight the so-called war on drugs. The prison industrial complex has fashioned and identified its surplus resource of bodies to keep this unholy operation energized.

Those occupying the lowest rung on the ladder of drug arrests receive the harshest punishments when it comes to participation in what is considered illegal contraband use or distribution. Our urban minority populations also have the distinguished dishonor of becoming the poster image of drugs in America. Interestingly, in one form or another our society is built on the production, selling, and use of chemical substances of one kind or another, be it legal or illegal. Drugs are a multibillion dollar a year Industry. Our economy would crumble without drug sales, both legal and illegal. Arrests and convictions of individual's accused of selling and/or buying illegal drugs are all part of what keeps the economy energized. Incarceration and subsequently community control of citizens keeps people working and allows states and counties to receive federal money. The individuals passing through the system are simply expendable. If one manages to fight his or her way free from this web of dishonor, another person is inserted in their place. This creates jobs as well as other forms of fiscal animation for the established culture.

It is an industry, and as with so many other industries, our youth have been structured into this industries revenue stream. And it is intentional! Heck, we are all a part of the system in one way or another! How do we impress upon young men that as a society we value them when another more salient reality is clubbing them upside the head, gunning them down and chocking them out?

I asked a young crack dealer that I had seen in a hood not far from a local house of worship if I could talk to him about why he sold drugs or how he got into that lifestyle. I told him I was writing a book about inner city youth and wanted his perspective. He was the type of individual that most people may know of, constantly out hustling, well known by police and neighborhood residents alike. Roughly 20 years old, he wore a black hoodie and blue jeans that drooped half way between his buttocks and his knees. He displayed tattoos across his hands and forearms and alongside his neck from his ear to his chest. He wore a pair of large studded earrings in his ears. As we talked he continuously puffed on a blunt, filling the air with the pungent smell of tobacco and marijuana. He spoke in a very intimidatingly harsh manner.

"I am seventeen and my mom's smoked dope and she sold dis shit to keep it floatin cause she ain't had no job or nuttin like dat." He said, *"An it was four a us in da house. I saw da money, it was good and shit. I wasn't tryin to be up in nobody's school and shit like dat."* I asked him if he ever wanted to become something else or do something positive with his life. *"Hell yea! I don't like dis'shit. My dude jus got popped three days ago by da dicks* (police). *I dam show ain't getting rich off dis'shit."* Why do you use so much profanity, I asked? *"Man, f--k you! And where the f--k is my money bitch?"* What money, I asked? *"I gave you da story now gimme my f--kin money dog."*

All the while I had the sense that this was an individual who could go off very quickly and become destructive, so I gave him ten dollars and walked away fast. It's not like I never knew anyone who sold drugs that would be safer to talk to. I wanted to be the man out on the street getting the fresh, unbiased opinion. I suppose I got that alright, and how!

Could this singular corner store dealer be a one-man operation? Or is he like the foreman of a company or maybe the rank and file worker who earns peanuts by comparison to the real king pin whose wealth grows exponentially — growing on the work and risk taken by the inner city grunts? The real drug dealer looks nothing like the young man I spoke to and is not found on the streets.

Who wants to be a slave? Raise your hand nice and high so we can see it! How about the overseer, who wants that job? How about plantation owner maybe? Don't be shy, step right up and name your game. If you don't speak up then we will have to assign a spot for you, or you may be left out of the game entirely and you don't want that so come on, step right up. Hmmm! A job is something we all need; we must all have a way of making a living and supporting ourselves and our families.

Communities are without a doubt interconnected and dependent upon each member as contributors. But how can we make living more equitable for those considered underclass? And can the field hand truly break free of the bonds of servitude to become what his or her heart desires and dreams, the dreams he or she aspires to reach while no one is around? The dreams that we all have late in the midnight hour as we lay our head down quietly on our pillow and imagine "What if?" Can the line from impoverishment to wealth be crossed by ordinary folk? We trade time and sweat for dollars and find that at the end of our work week we were only the middleman of sorts; receiving monies from our employer and passing it right along to the supplier of the goods and services necessary to stay in our homes.

We pay to live in our homes as a place to reside while we pay for our automobiles which takes us back and forth from home to work. We then obtain the money to do this again next week and the week after that ad infinitum until we pass away. Soon to be forgotten by our employer and leaving our job to the next fortunate soul who has been hoping to find a good job that has such good benefits. Remind me who won the civil war again; somehow it gets a little ambiguous sometimes.

Sidebar: *I am convinced that as a result of placing our priorities in order, obeying God, trusting in what He says about us, not what other people say about us, we move closer to truth. I believe that if we walk with integrity and right thinking anything* *is possible. All things are possible to them that believe. I am a positive thinker. Yet I see what's happening, which forces one to reexamine closely every belief and weighing them against certain realities.*

During the reconstruction era sharecropping became a way of life for many. The promise of hope and a chance for a better life came with the reality of despair and futility, crushing the dreams for many families looking for better days. Following the freeing of black slaves, sharecropping came to define the method of land lease that would eventually become a new form of slavery. Without land of their own, many blacks were drawn into this system where they worked a portion of the land owned by whites for a share of the profit from the crops. The poor blacks would receive all the seeds, food, and equipment they needed from the company store, which allowed them to run a tab throughout the year and to settle once the crops, which usually included cotton, were harvested.

When accounting time came, the black farmer was always a few dollars short of what he owed the landowner and the general store, so perpetually he began the New Year in greater debt. As the deficits grew, he found it not possible to escape from his circumstances within the parameters of law. Not to mention the Jim Crow laws that were in effect during this time. The hard, wearisome work led to stooped, physically destroyed, and psychologically shattered African Americans who could seldom envision escape for themselves or their children. The lives of these farmers were an endless round of poor diets, challenging weather, and figures at the company store that were unbeatable. Families with enough courage and help of abolitionists or other free-thinking citizens of the time escaped from the land owners during the blackness of night to the North where opportunities were believed to be better.

It seems that the fine print must be read and understood thoroughly and as any boxing fan knows, the final instruction before the fight begins is *"Protect yourself at all times."*

What does this all have to do with today's youth you may be asking yourself? One must always know where he or she is coming from in order to have a good, clear comprehension of the current heading upon which he or she is set. We must understand where we were in the past to figure if we are experiencing progress, regress, or no movement at all. Programs, operations, regulations, plotting of courses, plans and agendas do not just appear, they have purpose or functional intent. The Manual says the following in the book of Jeremiah, Chapter 29, verse 11: *"For I know the plans I have for you,' declares the Lord, 'plans to prosper you and not to harm you, plans to give you hope and a future.'"*

But who has programmed and planned a future of difficulty for us and our offspring? Who has planned that we be engaged in financial struggles for the entire duration of our adult lives? Whose plan is it that traps individuals with glitter, fresh paint, and flashy ads? As a society whose plan have we come into greater agreement with? Whose economic plan is employed with greater frequency in the world today, God's or the enemy's? The Manual says that we should give and it will be given back to us again in greater measure. The world says take by trickery and deceitful means. Hide the reality of the contract in the fine print section.

What will be the expected outcome if peace, prosperity, humility, truth, and godliness are whittled away bit by bit with each successive generation? As leaders let us look ahead with lucidity and understand that our actions or inactions impact future generations as they come behind us. Future generations are fully dependent upon the road we pave for them to travel on. History can prove to be a great indicator of future performance.

Each generation should be able to stand on the shoulders and the work of those that came before. Will the bridge we build now have sufficient integrity to bear the weight of our grandchildren and their children after them? Certainly, there are great people in each generational grouping. Presently we have outstanding role models such as former President and Michelle Obama, Colin Powell, Folorunsho Alakija, Shahrazad Ali, James Earl Jones, Will Smith, Oprah, Billy Graham, the Honorable Minister Louis Farrakhan and Mea Jemison, to name but a few. And we can continue to praise the examples set by the late Nelson Mandela and the late Maya Angelou. Nonetheless these great monuments of strength and courage cannot of themselves speak for the whole of a generation. The greatness of these and other iconic figures of our time in no way negates our responsibility to rise to meet our fullest potential. Only as a whole will the true message of our era be spoken.

Can we instruct our youth from a base of experience? Can we tell them that we have trusted God and kept His word and so should they? Can we say that we had principles and upheld them? Do our youth see us truly trusting God no matter what the circumstances may be? Whether we feel that we have been overlooked, beaten, or lied to, we must stand in faith. Whether we have received the credit we deserved for all the tireless hours we worked or not we must remain steadfast and resolute. God has stated in His word that we are to do good to those that hate us. These are some of the components of possessing a heart of godliness that we must leave behind as a road map for our youth to follow. Through heartache and pain, we toil on, through the fire of oppression and sickness we toil on. We also press through times of weakness as well as times of great strength. Some challenges come in the form of apparent success or prosperity. What and who we are on the inside is what is really on display. Angelic beings observe intently the great becoming of humanity. Also, our youth watch with great interest as we drum before them while they march.

Can we say with assurance that we have trusted God, and as a result witnessed miracles take place in our circumstances? A miracle is something that could not by any other means happen without divine intervention. Will we be able to tell the stories to our youth of how we gave God our all, reserving nothing, and believed His word against all odds, proving His word?

We must share these life experiences with our family, for we will overcome by the blood of the Lamb and by testimony. He suffered for our sake, and if you put your entire faith in Him you will likewise suffer, but a reward is waiting for those who trust in God in spite of danger, pain, threats of death, fear, or whatever the hardship may be. We must allow our youth to see God's work in our lives whether we're in the valley or on the mountain top. We must stop compromising our faith for dollars, prestige and pleasure. We must let the beacon light of God's power show forth through us to the next generation.

Live and Let Live

It is clear and evident that the world did not begin when I was born. Nor will the world end when I am gone. World shaping events, some good, some not so good, have been taking place all along from the beginning of time. There is no way to give emphasis to them all here now but I will talk about some that I have personally lived through and some that are close to the focus of this book.

Again, in the 1960s very interesting and sinister happenings occurred in this country. President John Fitzgerald Kennedy was shot and killed. Lee Harvey Oswald was accused of the slaying; an accusation that he vehemently denied. President Kennedy's 1963 assassination was one of the most shocking public events of the 20th century. He was, in my opinion, well loved by the vast majority of the nation which was evident by the outpouring of support and grief demonstrated by the American people when this tragedy occurred. Even as a young boy I was very pained by the loss of our president. The subsequent shooting of Lee Harvey Oswald by Jack Ruby further shrouded the incident in mystery, probably forever placing a question mark over the death of President Kennedy, fostering many conspiracy theories.

On February 21st, 1965 in Manhattan's Audubon Ballroom, Malcolm X, the prominent civil rights activist who I quoted earlier, was shot and killed. This great man, who rose to become one of the foremost American Muslim leaders and champions for civil rights, was assassinated. Once again conspiracy theories abounded.

Robert F. Kennedy successfully ran for senator of New York and in early 1968 Kennedy declared his candidacy for the U.S. presidency. He was shot and killed by Sirhan Sirhan at the Ambassador Hotel in Los Angeles on June 5th, 1968. RFK was not only a senator from New York, but also former President Kennedy's brother who was slain only five years earlier. Both Kennedy's were killed by what has been controversially debated ever since — a lone gunman's bullet or conspiracy? We may never know!

The 1960s was a time marked by revolution on every level. For example, Helen Gurley Brown's 1962 novel titled, *Sex and the Single Girl*, promoted premarital sex. This opened the door for many forms of sexually deviant behavior. Julio Caesar Chavez, in the early 1960s, formed the Migrant Farm Workers Union. During these times, the same type of push-back from the established culture was seen as in the Civil Rights movement. The conflict-ridden nature of this society became even more evident.

Hugh Hefner and the Playboy Empire tunneled great and lasting inroads to the undermining of moral integrity. His excavating under the surface of virtue, decency, and morality left us weaker spiritually as a nation. On August 9th, 1969, four of Charles Manson's followers brutally murdered Sharon Tate, her unborn baby, and four others who were visiting her. The following night, Manson's followers brutally killed Leno and Rosemary LaBianca in their home. The nation still rocking, was rolled again.

In 1963 Medgar Evers was murdered for speaking out against injustice. This sent another shiver up the spine of the consciousness of a nation already nearly knocked to the canvas from blow after blow of unrest. On June 21st, 1964, three young civil rights workers, a 21-year-old black Mississippian, James Chaney, and two white New Yorkers, Andrew Goodman, 20, and Michael Schwerner, 24, were murdered in Nashoba County, Mississippi. They had been working to register black voters in Mississippi during Freedom Summer and had gone to investigate the burning of a black church. They were arrested by the police on trumped-up charges. They were imprisoned for several hours, and then released after dark into the hands of the Ku Klux Klan, who beat and murdered them. It was later proven in court that a conspiracy existed between members of Neshoba County's law enforcement and the Ku Klux Klan to kill them.

On a very hot day, 101 degrees in June 1963, James Hood and Vivian Malone became the first two black students to enroll successfully at the University of Alabama. They suffered great humiliation and risk by standing against the National Guard and Governor George C. Wallace, Jr.'s symbolic and venomous stand in the schoolhouse door.

On April 4th, 1968, while standing on the balcony of the Lorraine Motel in Memphis, Tennessee, Dr. Martin Luther King, Jr. was assassinated with a gunman's bullet. Dr. Martin Luther King, Jr. was a civil rights leader who won the Nobel Peace Prize for his heroic efforts to bring piece and equality to a racially segregated nation embedded in the gridlock of hate. He was a prophet who declared future realities, some of which are now beginning to be realized and many that are yet stored in future treasure chests, awaiting upcoming generations to discover them. What strikes me as interesting is the timing of the events I have just described; they all took place within the short span of the 1960s. In the 230 years of our nation's history, in one decade we managed to forever alter the course of our future by slaying our leaders and prophets, and this by our own hand. These were not outside enemies that came upon our shores to destroy us from without, but as in biblical times, we killed our own deliverers.

The course of one's life can change dramatically with only one word or action, as I stated in the illustration about my football coach and his comment about my skinny neck. We must ask ourselves, are we today reaping what we see in many young lives that which we have sown many years ago? It's true that you reap later and greater than that which you have sown.

In any society, invariably we are all interconnected and interdependent upon one another. I am connected to the very first slave that set foot on American soil as well as I am connected to the one who brought him here. I am also connected to you and your great, great, great, grandchildren. I cannot act without, in some way, affecting you either now or forthcoming relatives of yours. We are all interconnected and what you do affects me either directly or indirectly, and will impact me sooner or later.

Sidebar: If we cut down a forest and build a parking lot, what have we truly gained? Is the tradeoff value significant enough to pay the price of destroying what is of benefit to the majority for the profit or desire of the few?

Do we truly know what the impact of extinguishing a life in progress has on future generations, especially a life that has previously demonstrated a recorded legacy of greatness along its continuum? What could we have gained as a society if we had not destroyed those treasured individuals who would lead us to a unity that we have not to date achieved?

Individuals who have positive influences on our nation, dedicated public servants with an understanding of what it takes to bring something good to our nation's people, should receive support — not death! When the Kennedys, King, and Malcolm X were assassinated, it appears as a nation we wholeheartedly turned the corner from innocence and idealism toward indecency and corruption. This turning point appears to be one from which we would not or could not deviate. We have pursued this malevolence with vigor on a scale of biblical proportions.

We chase wickedness not only nationwide, but globally as well as individually. It also appears that the same type of slaughter of those who were good for the masses has been taking place in times past from the beheading of John the Baptist to the crucifixion of Christ and the prophets of old. What about the way in which Abraham Lincoln died at the hand of Booth?

Mohandas Karamchand Gandhi, on January 30th, 1948, was walking toward his evening prayer meeting in front of a congregation of about 500 people when he was approached by a Hindu extremist named Nathuram Godse. Gandhi put his palms together in a traditional gesture of greeting. Godse pulled out a pistol and shot three bullets into Gandhi's chest at point-blank range. Momentarily, perhaps in shock or attempting to seek aid, Gandhi continued to move forward; then he crumbled to the ground and died.

Non-violence, peace, and living in quiet harmony with one's fellow man, we can't have that! Away, with those troublesome peacemakers, away with them all, right? Sure seems that way.

If we genuinely cared for others and passed the message of love down to our youth, and allowed them to perpetuate it and put their creative curve on it towards agreement instead of discord, how would the world look 40 years forward? I intentionally involved the time period of 40 years in this book because of the biblical significance of the number 40, notwith-standing it has been about 40 years since I myself was a public school student. Take out your Bible and study the corresponding instances of 40 being implicated in its pages which are listed below:

Israel in the wilderness, Deuteronomy 8:2-5; Psalm 95:10; Acts 13:18 (the third 40 of Moses' life, 120 years).

Judges 3:11, Under Barak, Judges 5:31, Under Gideon, Judges 8:28.

Forty Years of Probation under David, 2 Samuel 5:4.

Under Solomon, 1 Kings 11:42; Under Jeroboam II. See 2 Kings 12:17, 18; 13:3, 5, 7, 22, 25; 14:12-14, 23, 28.

Under Jehoash, 2 Kings 12:1; Under Joash; 2 Chronicles 24:1.

Forty Years of Probation by Humiliation and Servitude, Israel under the Philistines; Judges 13:1. 1 Samuel 4:18.

Israel Under Saul, Acts 13:21. 7:23. Moses in Midian, Acts 7:30, 40 Days

Forty days Moses was in the mount; Exodus 24:18; and to receive the Law; Exodus 24:18.

Forty days Moses was in the mount after the sin of the Golden Calf; Deuteronomy 9:18, 25

Forty days of the spies, issuing in the penal sentence of the 40 years; Numbers 13:26, 14:34.

Forty days of Elijah in Horeb; 1 Kings 19:8.

Forty days of Jonah and Nineveh; Jonah 3:4.

Forty days Ezekiel lay on his right side to symbolize the 40 years of Judah's transgression.

Forty days Jesus was tempted of the Devil; Matthew 4:2.

Forty days Jesus was seen of His disciples, speaking of things pertaining to God's Kingdom; Acts 1:2.

In the Bible, we often find instances where God made major changes and transformations after the period of 40. It rained for 40 days and 40 nights when God wanted to cleanse the world and start over. (Genesis 7:12) *"And the rain was upon the Earth 40 days and 40 nights."* Noah waited another 40 days after it rained before he opened a window in the Ark. (Genesis 8:6): *"And it came to pass at the end of 40 days, that Noah opened the window of the ark which he had made:"*

Embalming required 40 days (although this was an Egyptian custom, the Egyptians recognized the period of 40 for the preparation of going into a new life, which they called the afterlife). Moses was on the mountain with God for 40 days — twice! (Exodus 24:18) *"And Moses went into the midst of the cloud, and gat him up into the mount: and Moses was in the mount 40 days and 40 nights."* (Exodus 34:28-29) *"And he was there with the Lord 40 days and 40 nights; he did neither eat bread, nor drink water."* (Deuteronomy 10:10) *"Now I had stayed on the mountain 40 days and nights, as I did the first time, and the Lord listened to me at this time also. It was not His will to destroy you."*

It took the spies 40 days to search out the Promised Land and bring back fruit. (Numbers 13:25 KJV) *"And they returned from searching of the land after 40 days."* The Israelites spent 40 years in the wilderness, one year for each day they explored the Promised Land. (Exodus 16:35 KJV) *"And the children of Israel did eat manna 40 years, until they came to a land inhabited; they did eat manna, until they came unto the borders of the land of Canaan."* (Numbers 14:33-34) *"Your children will be shepherds here for 40 years, suffering for your unfaithfulness, until the last of your bodies lies in the desert. For 40 years — one year for each of the 40 days you explored the land — you will suffer for your sins and know what it is like to have me against you."*

As we find in 1 Samuel 17:16, for 40 days, twice a day, morning and evening, the Philistine giant named Goliath strutted in front of the Israelite army before being killed by David. Elijah strengthened by one angelic meal went 40 days to Mount Horeb where the Lord passed by and he heard the voice of God. (1 Kings 19:8) *"And he arose, and did eat and drink, and went in the strength of that meat 40 days and 40 nights unto Horeb the mount of God."*

Jonah warned the City of Nineveh they had 40 days until God would overthrow the city. The people repented in those 40 days and God spared the city. (Jonah 3:4 and 10) *"And Jonah began to enter the city a day's journey, and he cried, and said, yet 40 days, and Nineveh shall be overthrown. And God saw their works that they turned from their evil way; and God repented of the evil, that He had said that He would do unto them; and He did it not."*

Jesus fasted for 40 days in the wilderness. (Matthew 4:1-2) *"Then was Jesus led up of the Spirit into the wilderness to be tempted of the devil. And when he had fasted 40 days and 40 nights, He was afterward hungry."* Jesus was seen on the Earth 40 days after His crucifixion and resurrection. (Acts 1:3) *"After His suffering, He showed Himself to these men and gave many convincing proofs that He was alive. He appeared to them over a period of 40 days and spoke about the kingdom of God."* Let's borrow Mr. Peabody's Wayback Machine for a bit and look back in 40 year increments!

In the year 1776 the nation of the United States of America was founded. Forty years later in 1816 there was something called the year without summer. Many attributed this phenomenon to the sins of the people. This was a season in which the time of harvest and the warmth of the sun never fully came. Forty years later Dred Scott first went to trial to sue for his freedom in 1847. Ten years later, after a decade of appeals and court reversals, his case was finally brought before the United States Supreme Court. In what is perhaps the most infamous case in its history, the Court decided that all people of African ancestry, slaves as well as those who were free, could never become citizens of the United States and therefore could not sue in federal court. Needless to say, he remained a slave.

Roughly forty years after that Henry Ford drives his first Model-T through the streets of Detroit. I need not tell you how much this has helped to shape the course of humanity. Within the next 40 years we find ourselves in Nazi Germany during wartime. Earlier, in1936, Adolf Hitler turned his back so he need not witness Jessie Owens, the great African American track star, outpace his Arian brotherhood sprinters. We also find here that the "Final Solution" to what has been termed the Jewish problem is forged. Extermination of Jews had already begun in Germany during this time.

Once again back in Mr. Peabody's Wayback Machine we set the dial to 1976, 40 years after Jessie Owens embarrassed Hitler. In South Africa, Soweto riots mark the beginning of the end of apartheid. A tidal wave in Philippines kills 5,000. An Earthquake in Tabgshan, China kills 655,000. In Guatemala and Honduras an earthquake kills more than 22,000. Legionnaires Disease affects 4,000 delegates in Pennsylvania. In New York City, the "Son of Sam" pulls a gun and begins a series of attacks that terrorized the city for the next year. In the UK, the worst drought on record hits Britain. In the U.S. Hurricane Belle hits the East Coast.

Many speculate that these occurrences are acts of God maneuvering mankind toward its destiny. Forty appears to be of significance in Scripture and in recent history as well. It is my hope that we are embarking upon a season in which God will move on the behalf of our youth and bring about a time of renewal. Renewal which will bring the hearts and minds of our offspring closer to Him and unite peoples with each other in a more loving fashion. A time of renewal in which we will see the hearts of the sons return to fathers and daughters to their mothers.

War and Peace

In the United States, our arms buildup budget is massive. For example, the National Defense Budget Estimates for Fiscal Year 2015 shows a Total National Defense Budget of $636.6 billion[3]. National defense is something that no nation can afford to go cheap on. I get that part. As a world which may someday have to unite to defend itself against a common enemy not necessarily of this world, maybe we should utilize some "getalong" strategies with our neighbor. Maybe we should use monies and whatever else we can employ to make the world less hazardous and volatile. We're preoccupied with worry about individuals from across the water. Maybe we should start thinking about those who may come from or may have already come from across the great expanse of space. When I was born I knew nothing about the world or how I was supposed to behave. I was taught by parents, teachers, aunts and uncles and other adults:

"Repent ye this day or you shall surely burn in the flames of hells fire; live and let live; do your own thing; it's your life, live it to the fullest; get a good education; be kind to others; don't worry about nobody but yourself; its yo thang do what you wonna do I can't tell you who to sock it to; I'm black and I'm proud; if you're yellow you're mellow, if you're white you're alright, if you're brown stick around, but if you're black get back."

Countless scores of coded as well as obvious communications complicated how we relate to one another. Each of these messages had sort of a ring of truth to them as to how society operated on some level. As such they had to be weighed and measured.

Kids learn what is taught to them. If I see inappropriate behavior demonstrated every day without consequences leveled against the perpetrator, I would probably be more apt to behave inappropriately as well, and feel justified in doing so. What do I teach my son when he sees my behavior? How long will it take before he becomes what I am? Where will war and fighting end? Will we destroy all life on Earth? Or is it possible for us to show our youth another way to resolve conflict? Is there a way of reconciliation, a way of common good and allowing what's agreeable with me to be a resolution for you also? Our fore-parents made bombs; we made bigger, more powerful bombs. Our children will make even bigger and more powerful methods of killing than we made and their offspring will be off the chart with the ability to destroy each other.

Think of what the impact would be if we had a peace budget only a fraction of that of the war budget! Can we truly have thoughts of peace? Truth and freedom are free, contradictory to the notion that they are not.

Freedom is a space within the hearts and minds of each of us, the space where God is seated — or should be seated. Is it feasible in this day and age to believe that we can teach our youth a way of peace? Peace with their neighbor and peace as a worldwide concept. Or are we set upon a path of destruction and that's that? Must we pursue destruction to its logical conclusion? Will we have to allow our yet unborn grandbabies to reap the horror of our sowing and that of our forefathers?

While we're still on the topic of leadership, we must look at our nation's borders. Obviously, everyone knows that teenagers and preteens do not control our southern border, any of our many ports in Miami, or any other place where contraband may enter this nation. Youth do not control the illegal crossing of our borders by aliens seeking whatever it is they seek when they cross over. Young people today possess great intelligence and creativity on a level that previous generation could have only imagined. With the information age in full swing and at their fingertips, and having every form of electronic technology available to them, today's youth have skyrocketed to a new level of brilliance. How this brilliance is utilized is a topic for another day and time. It is my belief that the young people who many consider as the lost generation are simply committed to not becoming the exact image of their predecessors. To put it succinctly, they don't want to be like us!

We have developed into a society predicated on living by the propaganda of our own creation. We of the more mature sort have wondered precariously into a lifestyle of self-deception without taking cognitive recognition of its full ramifications. It's very simple to point the finger at the other group across the way. Although we may attempt to manage through the curtain of a modern — or new and improved lifestyle — outcomes are uncertain at best and a day of reckoning will one day this way come. I believe that we must look at ourselves before we look down on the youth. Whenever something is placed on our credit card, eventually the bill comes due. We have maxed out our card and the bill is in the mailbox. We have indeed accepted a false concept of what life is and embraced it without balking or hesitating. We have thrown caution to the wind, choosing that which will lead humankind into extinction if modifications are not made. The rap group, Public Enemy, told us *"Don't believe the hype;"* however, at this point we are believing our own hype "hook, line, and sinker," and passing it down stream to our youth, asking them to believe the hype also.

Sidebar*: It appears that for the survival of the human species there is an imbedded failsafe system which activates itself when uninterrupted termination sequence is put into operation and pursued either knowingly or unwittingly. New and fresh ideas brought from our youth may well be the saving grace of our nation and world, even life on Earth as we know it.*

There appears to be a departure from the dangerous course set so many generations ago. The impression of a new footprint in the hardened sod on the pathway to eternity has emerged. The plotting of a new route to ensure the survival of the human species is budding. This new course may appear even more dangerous, especially to those of us who have become com-fortable with the status quo politics and practices of our own making. Like in the movie *I ROBOT*, *V.I.C.K.I.* resolved that some men would have to be sacrificed to save the whole of mankind. Has some of our unprofitable ways become so cumbersome and dangerous that for the good of mankind upheaval and revolution of sorts must come to save a remnant. Could we be seeing the budding of this revolutionary ideation in today's youth? The oppressed have always revolted when conditions deteriorated to the point that they could no longer be tolerated. Gangsta rap, the thug mentality, the f--k the police attitude, and so many other countercultural ideals have crept into the psyche of our youth. I think it is very important and timely that we reach out to our youth and embrace them. Let them know that we love and accept them. We must be the best role models possible and restore the bridge between generations.

We can gain greater understanding of ourselves and thereby become able and ready to alter the legacy we leave with our sons and daughters by looking at ourselves straight on. Let's look through the lens of God's truth, not our contrived truth. If we honestly evaluate our actions and those of our forefathers in the light of blunt force candor, understanding what has happened and the impact it is having on families, communities, our nation and the world, we then gain greater perspective. I disapprove of and assail illegal as well as legal moral turpitude. Having looked at some of the issues that may cause youth to resist assimilation into current popular culture, let's continue to evaluate current trends with the understanding that we will bequeath the world to today's and tomorrow's youth. We must at all cost assist them in shaping a world that will be sustainable. Termination sequence must be interrupted!

Chapter Nine

The Appeal

The advent of crack cocaine and its impact on our society has been huge. Crack cocaine changed our nation. Most everyone knows someone whose life has been impacted by it. Our prisons are filled with individuals whose crime involved its use or distribution or possession. In the neighborhoods where it is bought and sold either in houses or on the street, families and children became expendable. It's not uncommon to have mothers walk to the crack houses three blocks over, intending to purchase and come right back to her two-year-old toddler. She instructs the baby to watch his three-month-old baby brother until she comes right back in five minutes. However well-intentioned, she ended up smoking at the crack house until morning. After running out of money she gave her body to buy more crack, only returning home the next morning empty, frustrated, and focused only on how to get more of the drug. This time her babies were safe at home. Their diapers now full, hungry and emotionally afraid, they had cried themselves asleep again.

Certainly, these two baby boys were ever so relieved to see their mom and looked forward to receiving her full attention now that she has come home. However, they received only the frustration of repeat performances of what they had experienced the night before — and the years roll on with little change! Of course, I fabricated these events as an illustration, but they are real in that very similar events commenced with the entrance of crack into our communities. Children like these two fictitious boys grow up like so many others, rarely having food in the home and frequently moving from one location to another due to evictions — often due to the fact the money was used for crack instead of the rent.

155

Fathers are anchors and stabilizing agents in family units. When we were children 40 years ago dads went to work and most moms stayed home and cared for the kids. Home was the place in which father, mother, and children ate together and watched TV together, and fathers were strong, influential figures. Now fatherhood is relegated to sitcom buffoonery. Too many fathers are absent from homes due to divorce, "playboyism," addictions and other miscreant behaviors. Let's look at drug addiction and fatherhood.

Stability is immediately lost to instability when the father is addicted. For many generations, in most African American families a strong, two-parent family was the gold standard. That standard is jeopardized when dad is "cracked." This places the family at risk of becoming fragmented and far less functional. Validation of the children is a most important function of fathers in a family unit. This function becomes less consistent because focus now is placed on drug-seeking behavior at the expense of the children's welfare. Subsequently, fathers in such circumstances who display sporadic attempts to guide or share concern for their families are viewed with skepticism by youth, and seen as contrived or counterfeit by mom. Dad is eventually rejected by mom and the children soon follow suit.

In time, students from such homes who may have otherwise performed well have a greater potential of failing in school. Without adequate social skills — which have not been taught at home — the better job prospects become less likely. Consequently, a cyclical outlook on life begins to instill itself within the next generation of that family.

In this condition, a family can get turned over to whatever opportunistic entity that may come along. Gang activity begins to look attractive, and if a gang is joined or not, the mindset to be sympathetic toward a gang way of life is often formed. The style of dress, music, people and places become common.

Opportunistic men move vicariously into the home setting with mom and the children. Such men have no genuine ties to the youths in the family, so abuse is more likely to occur. Seeing dad only sporadically, his influence is still large, but in a negative way. His drug emaciated mind and body communicates ostentatiously adverse and harmful messages to the children.

Fathers are very important members of any family setting. Fathers guide the family either precariously in error or by providing structure and correctness. Our formative years do impact the choices we make and the direction we take as teens and young adults.

God works things out generationally! Hebrews 3:10 says, *"That is why I was angry with that generation, and I said, 'their hearts are always going astray, and they have not known my ways.'"*

Understand that our enemy chips away slowly, generation after generation, also almost subliminally and imperceptibly. One must view from a macro perspective to be able to see his handy work more clearly. We must take the loftier vantage point, where over long stretches of time, people and cultures we can view with greater perceptiveness. Understanding one's family history is of great help when considering these matters. The micro view is of no use and must be discarded when looking at the work of the enemy. We cannot allow ourselves to enter the trap of only seeing ourselves in the capsule of today. We must see ourselves as God sees us and take the measures He commands to stay focused. We must view ourselves from years past as well as in today and tomorrow, next week, next year, and so on. It would be beneficial to maintain a journal and make accurate records of what is taking place in one's family history and in your life, making note of all appearance of causal links between events and outcomes. What appears to be a coincidence or casual occurrence may not be so coincidental or casual. Something we, our parents or ancestors may have set in motion may now be materializing in our current circumstances.

According to *Science Daily*[1] (September 8, 2007), *"Following a decline of more than 28 percent, the suicide rate for 10- to-24-year-olds increased by 8 percent, the largest single-year rise in 15 years, according to a report just released in the Centers for Disease Control and Prevention's (CDC) Morbidity and Mortality Weekly Report (MMWR). The decline took place from 1990 to 2003 (from 9.48 to 6.78 per 100,000 people), and the increase took place from 2003 to 2004, (from 6.78 to 7.32), the report said."*

It was further noted that, *"This is the biggest annual increase that we've seen in 15 years. We don't yet know if this is a short-lived increase or if it's the beginning of a trend,"* said Dr. Ileana Arias, director of CDC's National Center for Injury Prevention and Control. *"Either way, it's a harsh reminder that suicide and suicide attempts are affecting too many youth and young adults. We need to make sure suicide prevention efforts are continuous and reaching children and young adults."*

Our young people need to feel our loving hand on them. Moreover, through us as a primary route, we must insure that they experience God's loving hand on them as well. We must lead them by example and by experience with our love and kindness. Why would young people want to do away with themselves? What conditions could be so strenuous that the option of death would seem to be the better choice? Could a parent perhaps intervene and disrupt such a thought cycle that would lead a young person to suicide? We haven't been as successful as we could have been with imparting faith into following generations if suicide looks good to so many of our kids. Mental illness may lay under the surface within the minds of many suicides; however, some have no hope, or a lack of faith that things can or will get better. Were we provided with a full measure of faith by watching our forefather's lives? Were you? At some point, we must by all means and at all cost assume the responsibility of getting whatever needs to be done, done. This is not to absolve youth of any responsibility for their behaviors or their own choices. We must simply provide all the tools needed for them to perform tasks effectively, thereby building hope and faith in tomorrow.

Government policies have given us much to be concerned about as well. We can clearly understand that many of our politicians are not at all interested in service to their constituency; instead, their primary concern seems to be re-election. They legislate policies that restrict and trap individuals. They make policies that serve their own purposes or that of the power elite. Are our youth supposed to be completely blind to these realities? What is the message that could be received by such dealings? What are youths learning from this? Again, remember we have very intelligent young people. Possibly they could learn that it's all about the money baby! Don't care who you hurt, just get paid. Did our kids not see the news reports of the Enron scandal? Of course they did! What about the giant shopping supercenter crushing the competition without any concern for those who lose their jobs in competing companies? Remember, *"Resistance is futile, you will be assimilated."* So says the Borg, in *Star Trek: The Next Generation,* as they arrive on the scene in a hostile takeover of all operations. You all know which giant Mart with the large blue sign above the entranceway I am alluding to. As a result, people are losing their homes and other property. The merchandise is being manufactured in overseas sweatshops, and the little guy is taking it on the chin again and again while the bully continually takes all the milk money on the business playground.

It's as if you can hear it clearly said in the board meeting: *"We don't care, just get the money."* Now, where else have I heard that statement made? It's more than just a statement, it's a prevailing attitude which crosses all cultural, economic, religious, social, political, corporate and all other lines. I heard that statement made when I talked to that young drug dealer on the street near the local house of worship; yea, that's it! I wonder how he and so many others developed this philosophy. I believe that gradually and inconspicuously this mindset crept into a large part of society's neural pathways.

Adults are teachers and leaders of youthful minds, just as it has always been. Nothing has really changed in that regard. As a matter of fact the Manual says in Ecclesiastes, 1:1-11: *"The words of the Teacher, son of David, king of Jerusalem: 'Meaningless! Meaningless!' says the Teacher. 'Utterly meaningless! Everything is meaningless.' What does man gain from all his labor at which he toils under the sun? Generations come and generations go, but the Earth remains forever. The sun rises and the sun sets, and hurries back to where it rises. The wind blows to the south and turns to the north; round and round it goes, ever returning on its course. All streams flow into the sea, yet the sea is never filled up. To the place the streams come from, there they return again. All things are wearisome, more than one can say. The eye never has enough of seeing, nor the ear its fill of hearing. What has been will be again, what has been done will be done again; there is nothing new under the sun. Is there anything of which one can say, 'Look? This is something new?' It was here already, a long time ago; it was here before our time. There is no remembrance of men of old, and even those who are yet to come will not be remembered by those who follow."*

I am appealing to the part of you that wants righteousness and goodness to march on now and when we are gone. I am appealing to those who desire godliness in their own lives and their children's offspring's lives as well. I am talking to those that desire the world to be filled with God's goodness. Those who never thought much about it, I'm asking you now to think soberly about the future of humanity where your lineage will exist. And to those who are contrary to godliness, I ask you to scientifically deduce whether it's better that we support living together in harmonious unity or to jeopardize human existence on the Earth? Is it better to walk in harmony with good or continue to walk in rebellion? We are leaders and instructors; our youth watch our lives as we demonstrate for them.

As leaders and instructors, are we clarifying for our students or are we confusing them? Everyone knows that to pervert what is natural and in its place cling to a distorted representation of reality is purely confusion. We have priests who are set in place to provide spiritual direction taking sexual advantage of young boys in places designated for sacred worship.

The ordination to high offices in the church of some who openly practice homosexuality obviously cries out there is something ill fitted. Yet we continue to pursue this course. We have gone to such an extreme that if one were even to speak out against such perversions it is considered hate or intolerance. The person who speaks out against perversion is held up to ridicule and scorn, but this distorted practice of misuse is somehow upheld or swept under the carpet. Justice is purchased in courtrooms on a regular basis.

We are very tricky in our advertising to the point of overtly lying about the products we're pitching. Daily business rip-offs are now the norm. We justify and make legal the killing of unborn babies, but if we harm a dog, a duck, or a kitten, that's a crime for which the offender can be fined or jailed. We have extreme fighting on TV with men or women beating each other to a bloody pulp. People sit as spectators of this cruel blood sport, cheering or booing the competitors without an iota of recognition of the societal hypocrisy before them. But if we allow dogs to fight in this manner we would be stripped of our NFL or other career and thrown into prison.

Obviously, something's wrong and it appears to be a heart or spiritual condition.

The Manual says that there would come a time upon the Earth that right would be considered wrong and wrong would be called right; most certainly we have come to such a threshold.

Truth is now relative and subject to one's own interpretation. Stealing is a common practice. Murder, assaults and misconduct of all sorts are everyday occurrences. Our court rooms and jail facilities are overflowing and we report that we are more liberated today than in previous times. We are great thinkers nowadays; we can navigate our own path without the aid of anyone else. We captain our own ship and are the masters of our own destiny. As a society, we say by our actions that *"We need no assistance from an unseen God who is a subjective figure anyway; one we can't see, touch, or intellectually relate to. Such is barbaric, uncivilized, and certainly beneath us who have become so enlightened, right?"* Be your own man; pull yourself up by your bootstraps; don't be dependent upon anyone else! *"You do you, and I'll do me!"* There is no such thing as right or wrong; it's all good as long as you feel good about it!

However, if you were an architect or an engineer and you built a road that led from point A to point Z and you had signs posted for me to make it successfully from the beginning of the road to my ultimate destination, would you provide me with a clear map and signs which I could read? Would the signs clearly indicate to me where to turn right or left? Where to stop and where to speed up? Or would the signs and map be up to my interpretation and I could take it to mean anything I wished it to mean?

Again, what is the message our youth receive from the confusing signs we set out for them to follow? We are to protect, instruct, lead, guard, provide safety, nurture, and care for our young. Who would give their child a stone if he asked you for bread? The mighty eagle feeds her young until it's time for them to leave the nest, then she teaches them to sore high above the lowly ground dwellers. Yet we as God's most cherished creation choose to perform well below model standards and teach our young to follow suit. The most common of beasts protect and care for their young until they are old enough to care for themselves. Every individual set of circumstances are obviously viewed separately and are taken on their own merit. Certainly, all cases are not the same. However, the human condition has demonstrated a recorded history of allowing its base or less honorable qualities to lead the way while the more admirable traits appear dormant.

As I begin to conclude I am reminded of a story I heard as a child. From the story, *The Emperor's New Clothes,* may I now offer plausible insights taken from this poignant story and apply them to the topic we are discussing? In the story, the Emperor had been duped into believing that the fabric of his very, very fine suite of clothing was so grand that only the most cultured person could see it. Conversely, the truth was that there was no fabric. The devious tailor only simulated fabric for the Emperor's ego. After his fabulous suit was complete as per the dubious tailor's instructions, the Emperor had his suit put on himself and he paraded down Main Street naked as a Jaybird, believing that he had on the finest set of clothes that only truly cultured people could see. The Emperor was unable to bring himself to admit that he couldn't see anything himself because he wanted to be the most cultured of all because, after all, he was the Emperor!

Well, as the story proceeds, a ruddy young boy was in the crowd that day. This is simply conjecture on my part but, I would theorize that such a boy had no formal training in etiquette. As the story is told he was alone without his parents or adult guidance as well. This uneducated, uncultured brat told it as he saw it when he saw the naked Emperor. Inquisitively he stated, *"But he isn't wearing anything at all."* Others who were not speaking up prior to this boy's statement for fear of not being considered high class citizens, began to whisper, *"Yes he is naked alright."* Now mind you, everyone could see that the Emperor was naked all along, but refused to announce it. Why? They also had a deep need to feel they were well suited to be considered high class. As the story is told, once the Emperor's shame had been revealed he went forward, even more determined to finish his promenade down Main Street. I'm sure perspiration was popping off his royal brow like water over Niagara Falls as his embarrassment grew, he realized all could see his nakedness. He knew that he had been duped into believing that he had on fine apparel. Ultimately, he had to admit what he must have suspected all along, that he was indeed naked. Undoubtedly, the Emperor knew of his obvious condition all along, but allowed himself to become self-deluded based on self-absorption or a self-righteous desire to feel superior.

I can draw several presumptions from this story which applies to our present topic. We see the greed, lack of compassion, divorce rate, political and every other kind of corruption, sexual perversions and promiscuity so prevalent today. We also see the prevalence of drug and alcohol use, religious schemes, and everybody trying to grab their piece of the pie at the expense of providing our youth with the compassion, real love, and proper guidance that they need and deserve. We must give our time, talent, money, love, and commitment to those whose care we have been charged with. This also raises a straight-to-the-point question: has the youth of today, as the boy in the story *The Emperor's New Clothes,* stood together to declare that with our present day cultural norms there is nothing to see, our generation is in large part naked?

"Therefore, away with them! I have no respect for what they stand for or who they think they are, and I don't give a f--k what they think." Wow! There's that term again! I have heard so many young people say that, but what are they really saying to us when we hear that phrase? Some more respectful youth just say, *"I don't care,"* but others say it with the more graphic expression. What should we conclude because of such an attitude?

If you look and listen to the way the train rolls down the track of life, you can hear that same statement growing louder and louder as time moves forward, and the station for the last stop begins to come into view. Clickity clack, clickity clack, the train rolls on. Clickity clack, clickity clack, clickity clack, year after year, with steam billowing out of the stack, you hear it coming down the tracks to the end times. The subdued, sleepy-eyed feelings which long trips produce, now are giving way to restlessness and agitated anticipation of disembarking at the last scheduled stop.

You know how it feels when you begin a long road trip; the excitement of leaving home is a different kind of excitement than that of reaching your destination. As the race of humanity, we set out on a trip so long ago, and now we are beginning to see the road signs telling us that our destination exit ramp is coming up soon. As with visiting my cousins in Cincinnati, Ohio as kids, we all got sleepy during the long drive. But when we saw the road sign while traveling South on I-71 indicating that Montgomery road was only a few miles away, everyone began to anticipate getting out of the car and seeing our beloved relatives. Humanity, I believe, is feeling that same type of agitated anticipation and the mental preparations to get out of the vehicle too. Those same restless symptoms are beginning to emerge. Youth are like our dash indicators, telling if there is trouble on board; they show how much gas is left in the tank; how fast we are going; distance to final destination; if our oil is low or are we running hot? We need to pay attention to these sensitive instruments.

The lyrics to the 1960s hit by The Who, called "My Generation," had somewhat of an appeal to the youth of that era. They did not want to become what they envisioned as the establishment generation. The Who is an English rock band formed in 1964, with vocalist Roger Daltrey, guitarist Pete Townsend, bassist John Entwistle, and drummer Keith Moon. They became known for energetic live performances which often included instrument destruction. As lead singer Roger Daltrey stutters the words in unprecedented rock band genius, it is clear that the generation being talked about in his song is struggling to be heard and understood, but not quite able to break through with the type of clarity necessary for their counterparts to receive them as they needed to be understood.

Destroying the musical equipment as the show came to its climax was in my view indicative of the rebellious nature of the times in which this generation came up and their unwillingness to go along just to get along. In this song Daltrey proclaims that people try to put them *"d- d- down"* while the rest of the band harmonize, talking about my generation. He says that things do look awful *"c-c-cold"* and he hopes he dies before he gets old. It sounded to me like he never wanted to become what he perceived the older generation to be.

While the young boy in the story of *The Emperor's New Clothes* made his discovery apart from his parents, can we also see our youth making self-directed decisions without us? Perhaps they do so because we have at some point allowed them to be without our unbroken guidance and our consistent presence, and now it's too late to put the horse back into the barn? And finally, if indeed we are in some way naked, who outfitted us with a suit of nothing? Why do we continue to wear it like the Emperor, steadily strolling down the promenade path knowing full-well that we are naked? Are we without proper attire because of our greed, passions, and lusts? In what other areas could we cover our shame and be more outfitted with humility and temperance? Consequently, if any of these presumptions are in any way valid, will we admit in sufficient numbers as adults that we are naked and begin clothing our nakedness before our youth? Remember that Canaan was cursed due to his father Ham looking upon his father Noah's nakedness. Read the account in the Book of Genesis, 9:20-28.

World Views, Old News

America was, once upon a time, very well loved and Americans were well received abroad. Now it seems as if we are hated and viewed with loathing or indifference by many other nations who would do away with us all if they could. When did we become foes to so many?

Where does terrorist ideology come from and why are they so focused on us lately? Are their differences of philosophical views growing out of utter madness on their part? It's barbaric and criminal to kill because of ideological differences. We must unequivocally uphold the preciousness and sanctity of life and liberty. The great land of America was founded upon high moral and Godly principals. Such principals being based on biblical fundamentals with which we now only placate ourselves, as if we as a nation still honored them.

Such moral principles are strangely missing from our policies and practices today. How can we who began with such a high moral inaugural launch, now be called the "Great Satan?" Surely, we must be aware that not all but many of our Western views, business and politics, as well as many other practices we immerse ourselves in, are fatally flawed. Ask yourself, why do those we consider crazy around the world hate us so? Why is there so much anti-American sentiment in the world today? Should it be an area of our concern to the degree that we as the American people will do what is necessary to resolve the issues within ourselves individually and collectively? Obviously, we can't just join a, *"You bomb me and I'll bomb you back"* game.

Is there anything we can focus on individually or jointly as citizens or policy makers that will answer these questions? Is there anything that ordinary folk like you and me can do to assuage some of the anti-Americanism seen globally? Government will not or cannot correct what has gone amiss. This is a "people issue" and we need to look very seriously at ourselves for answers. War cannot solve present situations; we have always had wars and rumors of wars and nothing is resolved to the extent that peace rains over the landscape. Allowing ourselves to be systematically blown up by our enemies till we are all gone isn't going to work either. Neither can we acquiesce or concede to the demands of those who desire to have us dead. People issues and heart conditions require God totally in order that our issues come to be resolved.

I am not suggesting that Americans bear the weight of international incongruity alone, but that each man and woman cleans his or her own side of the street and hold our legislators accountable for foreign policies that are not wise, calling for them to be replaced with wiser strategies. There must come a time in one's lifetime when soul searching and reconciliation take place. Regarding this topic, the alternative is unacceptable and cannot be allowed to continue to blossom.

Terrorism on American soil has been established and has been ongoing for many years. The number of attacks along with the severity of destruction of lives and property appears to be increasingly shocking and disturbing. Are we at all interested in why such hatred for us exists? Do we ever ask ourselves if we could have done something to provoke any of the hostility? Or shall we continue to maintain that others are just crazy and we have no culpability in these matters?

African American citizens have been assimilated into the main stream of our culture to the extent that we share and advance many of its ideologies.

Just a few short generations ago America dealt with us very poorly. This is not to say that America loves black people now, clearly it does not. Nonetheless we have become a part of America to the degree that we have forgotten what we've endured here. We are not outraged when the same system that mistreated us moves abroad to ensnare others.

What social and economic platforms did America stand on? It stood on us. It bombed our churches, our homes and our schools as well as lynched our young men. Has such an entrenched mentality of superiority and dominance subsided or has it simply assimilated and expanded abroad? Have we too become part of the oppressive machinery just like early America? They couldn't see that subjugation bruises those who fall under its weight. Now, after we have fine jobs, homes, cars and expendable cash on hand also, have we also become blind? The following incidents are listed as an indication of the fact that enemies have infiltrated our communities and neighborhoods, living among us as fellow citizens but awaiting opportunity to destroy us. Consider the following:

4/14/1972, New York, NY: Ten members of a local mosque phone in a false alarm and then ambushed responding officers, resulting in the death of one officer.

7/18/1973, Washington, DC: Nation of Islam members shoot seven members of a family to death in cold blood, including four children.

10/19/1973, Oakland, CA: Nation of Islam terrorists kidnap a couple and nearly decapitate the male hostage; they raped the woman and left her for dead.

10/29/1973, Berkeley, CA: One person was killed when a woman is shot repeatedly in the face by terrorists.

11/25/1973, Oakland, CA: A grocer is killed in his store by terrorists.

12/11/1973, Oakland, CA: A man is killed by terrorists while using a telephone booth.

12/13/1973, Oakland, CA: A woman is shot to death on the sidewalk by terrorists.

12/20/1973, Oakland, CA: Terrorists gun down an 81-year-old janitor.

12/22/1973, in Oakland, CA: Terrorist kills two people in separate attacks in one day.

12/24/1973, Oakland, CA: A man is kidnapped, tortured and decapitated by terrorists.

1/24/1974, Oakland, CA: Four people died in five vicious shooting attacks by terrorists. One was left paralyzed for life. Three of the victims were women.

4/1/1974, Oakland, CA: A terrorist shoots two members of the Salvation Army; killing a man and injuring a woman.

4/16/1974, Ingleside, CA: A man is killed while helping a friend move past terrorists.

3/9/1977, Washington, DC: Terrorists storm three buildings and hold 134 people hostage. At least two innocent people were shot; one died.

7/22/1980, Bethesda, MD: A political dissident is shot and killed in front of his home by an Iranian agent who was an American convert to Islam.

8/31/1980, Savoy, IL: An Iranian student shoots and kills his next door neighbors, a husband and wife.

1/31/1990, Tucson, AZ: A Sunni cleric is assassinated in front of a Tucson mosque after declaring that two verses of the Qur'an were invalid.

11/5/1990, New York City, NY: An Israeli rabbi is shot to death by a terrorist attacker at a hotel.

1/25/1993, Langley, VA: Two CIA agents are gunned down outside of their headquarters by a Pakistani affiliated with the Mujahedeen.

2/26/1993, New York, NY: Terrorists detonate a massive truck bomb under the World Trade Center in an attempt to collapse the towers. Six people are killed and over 1,000 are injured.

3/1/1994, Brooklyn, NY: Terrorists fire on a vanload of Jewish boys, killing one.

4/19/1995, Oklahoma City, OK: The Federal Government complex located downtown was bombed, killing 168 people.

3/23/1997, New York, NY: A Palestinian leaves an anti-Jewish suicide note behind and travels to the top of the Empire State building where he shoots seven people in a bloody attack. Six are injured and one is killed in this attack.

4/3/1997 Lompoc, CA: A prison guard is stabbed to death by a radical Muslim.

10/31/1999, Nantucket, MA: An Egyptian airline pilot runs a planeload of 217 passengers into the water after uttering a prayer, killing all on board.

3/17/2000, Atlanta, GA: A local spiritual leader shoots to death a deputy sheriff and injures his partner.

9/11/2001, Washington, DC: One hundred and eighty four people are dead and 53 are injured when hijackers steer a passenger airliner into the Pentagon.

9/11/2001, Shanksville, PA: Forty airline passengers are killed after hijackers attempt to fly the plane into the U.S. Capitol building, but it crashes before reaching its destination.

9/11/2001, New York, NY: Two thousand seven hundred and seventy two people were killed and 251 injured when Islamic hijackers fly two planes packed with fuel and passengers into the Twin Towers of the World Trade Center.

3/19/2002, Tucson, AZ: A 60-year-old man is gunned down by Muslim snipers on a golf course.

5/27/2002, Denton, TX: Snipers kill a man as he works in his yard.

7/4/2002, Los Angeles, CA: A man pulls out a gun at the counter of an Israeli airline and kills two people.

9/5/2002, Clinton, MD: A 55-year-old pizzeria owner is shot six times in the back by terrorists at close range.

9/21/2002, Montgomery, AL: Snipers shoot two women, killing one.

9/23/2002, Baton Rouge, LA: A Korean mother is shot in the back by terrorist snipers.

10/2/2002, Wheaton, MD: Terrorist snipers gun down a program analyst in a store parking lot.

10/3/2002, Montgomery County, MD: Snipers kill three men and two women in separate attacks over a 15-hour period.

10/9/2002, Manassas, VA: A man is killed by snipers while pumping gas two days after a 13-year-old is wounded by the same team.

10/11/2002, Fredericksburg, VA: Another man is killed by terrorist snipers while pumping gas.

10/14/2002, Arlington, VA: A woman is killed by terrorist snipers in a Home Depot parking lot.

10/22/2002, Aspen Hill, MD: A bus driver is killed by terrorist snipers.

8/6/2003, Houston, TX: After undergoing a religious revival, a Saudi college student slashes the throat of another student with a 4" butterfly knife, nearly decapitating the young man.

12/2/2003, Chicago, IL: A terrorist doctor deliberately allows a patient to die from an easily treatable condition.

6/16/2006, Baltimore, MD: A radical man runs down five strangers with a car.

6/25/2006, Denver, CO: A 62-year-old moviegoer is shot to death by a terrorist.

10/6/2006, Louisville, KY: In an "honor attack," a terrorist rapes and beats his estranged wife, leaving her for dead, then savagely murders their four children.

2/13/2007, Salt Lake City, UT: A terrorist immigrant goes on a shooting rampage at a mall, targeting people buying Valentine's Day cards at a gift shop, killing five.

1/1/2008, Irving, TX: A terrorist immigrant shoots his two daughters to death because they adopted a "Western lifestyle."

7/6/2008, Jonesboro, GA: A deranged man strangles his 25-year-old daughter in an "honor killing."

2/12/2009, Buffalo, NY: The founder of a terrorist sympathetic TV station beheads his wife in the hallway for seeking a divorce.

6/1/2009, Little Rock, AR: A terrorist with "religious motives" shoots a local soldier to death inside a recruiting center.

11/2/2009, Glendale, AZ: A father drives his car over his daughter and kills her because she has become "too Westernized!"

11/5/2009, Ft. Hood, TX: A U.S. Army psychiatrist, Major Nidal Malik Hassan, shoots to death 13 unarmed soldiers and wounds 31 others while yelling praises to Allah.

(https://www.thereligionofpeace.com/attacks/american-attacks.aspx / For more information visit this website)

This is just a small sampling of such acts that have taken place on American soil. The point is that America is not as well loved as it has been in the past. What we must ask ourselves is, why? As we can see from the many, many attacks committed here on American soil, our enemies are among us, and they are committed to their cause. Our cause as a nation is, or should be, one that we are equally, if not more fervently, committed to, than our enemies. I believe that right is on our side, and should be upheld by us as individual citizens. We must rise to a new level of accountability. Together we must climb out of the mud of dishonor and demonstrate to our youth — and to the world — that we are collectively worthy of the trust placed in us to defend this great land God has provided.

Speculation as to some of the causes behind the anti-American sentiment worldwide could be found in our spiritual, political, social, and economical beliefs. Such a position may all stem from a single source, a less than all-inclusive source.

I'm referring to a source which generates much confusion and division, a source that the Manual has warned us to guard against. It's a source that keeps us at odds with one another. A source we utilize to exclude others around us, and a source that is at the very core of many other ills within our daily lives, and indeed the world as we know it. This source is one which can stymie one's ability to deliberate in a collective or cooperative fashion. This view would only allow for an individual to approach ideas and imaginings from a short-sighted perspective.

This particular source would leave our youth at a specific disadvantage due to resource depletion. This resource depletion is brought about by our time, money, attention, affection, energy, deep concern and greater love being expended on "me, myself, and I."

It appears that selfishness is at the core of most of today's problems. When I am more focused on my career, my spouse, my god (or idol), my sports team, my drug, my church or religion, my car, my music, my TV program, my political views, my recreation, and my children without concern for yours, there is a problem. There are so many other things that can be put between me and my neighbors, or between the youth and the world around them. What is the unspoken but very loud message being sent? Knowing where you belong and then being there, as I stated earlier, is an essential component to wellness in a family or community. Providing clear, unambiguous indicators between generations makes available greater opportunity for future generations to move smoothly in the direction of righteousness, decency, and morality. Conversely, confusing and misleading indicators place our youth at risk of falling prey to all types of opportunistic entities that are waiting just around the corner for them to arrive unprepared. The downside is that our nation could sink to unparalleled moral and spiritual decay. This would bring ruin to our society if we cannot make the necessary modifications before we reach the point of no return.

Sidebar: In sporting events, there are regulation time periods, at the end of which the ball either goes to the other team, the period ends, or the game is over. Life is somewhat like that in many respects. What would happen if we do not make the necessary substitutions and adjustments before the specified time period that only God himself knows, runs out?

As the so-called "world leader," our nation has a greater responsibility to be morally accountable. What is the benefit of leading if we lead amiss? If the blind lead the blind, everyone falls into a ditch.

Every great civilization that has ever fallen has collapsed first from within. In some instances the final blow eventually came from without. The upshot to growing in an atmosphere of genuine love and willingness to give according to the currency set forth in the Manual of truth will allow for a world which perpetuates seed time and harvest where the harvest is something good and plentiful.

The first root or tree which bore the fruit of righteousness being the ALMIGHTY who brought forth His first born into humanity, which is Christ the anointed one. Christ became the seed which, when planted in the Earth, brought forth much more fruit of moral fiber. You are being fashioned into His image, identifying yourself as lifeless to respond to the secular demands of your flesh, are planted as a seed also. Once springing forth through the hard soil of life you bring additional fruit, our youth.

It is a good and plenteous harvest that, when reaped, will bring in the greatest bumper crop of all time. We have been called "infidels" and the "Great Satan" by some who dislike us. Conversely, we view them in that same light. Clearly, some soul searching and realignment of truths and focus shifting must take place on both sides of that coin. As parents, community and religious leaders, state and national political figures, or any other leaders, we must lead, follow, or get the heck out of the way! Time is of the essence and we have no more of it to waste.

There are many good leader's worldwide that we must hear and allow them to help us rethink some of the old, antiquated, unworkable ideas and methods. There are parents who have cogent, logical, rational methods of raising youth. There must be a platform for reproducing on a national level, their sound, proven approaches to communication with youth. Of necessity, those among us with wisdom regarding self-management must have their opportunities to help those of us who struggle.

This is no time to hold on to the notion that if we continue to force what clearly doesn't fit, that one day it will. It's time to be honest with ourselves and shed unprofitable methods and seek out those that bring healing, restoration and clarity. We've all seen the wrist bands asking, what would Jesus do? Let's not only see that as a clever saying but truly consider it as our path also.

Chapter Ten

Hold Your Horses

What would be some of the possibilities of pursuit that we could employ to turn these situations from what we see today into positives for our youth, as well as the larger society considering that the world itself will be bequeathed to those who follow us? The Earth is the Lord's and the fullness thereof and all that dwell in it are His as well. Nevertheless, our future as a human race will be lived out through our offspring, those who come after us.

Some years ago, the news reported that an 18-year-old American citizen by the name of Michael Peter Fay pled guilty in a Singapore court to vandalizing cars. This young man from St. Louis, Missouri, pled guilty to two charges of vandalism involving spray-painting cars, two counts of mischief for throwing eggs at cars, and one count of possession of stolen property. He was sentenced to six strokes from a rattan, which is a type of cane or switch. This form of caning, or flogging, is public punishment designed to discourage future occurrences by the offender. The judge who passed the sentence on Fay included a hefty fine as well.

Now this is just speculation on my part, but I can see Fay and his friends, if he did not act alone, going through various neighborhoods, possibly having alcohol and/or other substances in their systems, full of euphoria, laughing and carousing in their revelry. I can further envision that no real harm was meant to be inflicted by Fay, just youthful mischief. However, just as with everything else, there is another side to be considered, such as damaging another person's personal property, the breaking of the law, and the penalty that one is responsible to pay if apprehended.

Fay was caned as his punishment on May 5, 1994. As stated earlier, caning is a form of flogging or severe spanking in which a person would receive a specified number of sharp strikes to the buttocks area with a type of bamboo cane or rod. In Fay's case, a rattan was employed. In Singapore caning is a punishment that the public may witness. While caning may be extreme or harsh by today's standards, I'll bet Fay did not become a repeat offender!

Sidebar: *"Spare the rod and spoil the child!" This common saying has been adapted from the Bible, Proverbs 13:24, where we find the following: "He that spareth his rod hateth his son: but he that loveth him chasteneth him betimes."*

In public schools, right here in America we once had paddling or swats, as it was called by us students. As a child, I remember that there were times when our parents even took a belt, or what we called a switch, from a particular type of tree and used it to discipline wayward children. Imagine that, parent's disciplining their children! What a retro concept! Sounds like we are once again in Sherman and Mr. Peabody's Wayback Machine!

When I was a child and mom and dad told us to go to bed, we simply went upstairs. There were five of us: two girls and three boys. We played, jumped in the beds, quarreled, and yelled out of the windows to our friends who got to stay outside much later than we did. Many a night it became necessary for our parents to bring a switch or belt upstairs and it was "whack, whack, whack," on our "back, back, back;" meaning our back-side. It seems we tested the boundaries of the set parameters. I believe it is a symptom of the human condition to gauge parameter integrity. It's also reassuring to understand where lines are drawn. Either we needed to feel the restraining wall of our parent's guidelines or we were just testing the boundaries. We knew what would eventually happen if we persisted!

Another youthful yearning is to seek love in the form of restraint. Although this can be on a subconscious level, it's real nonetheless. Once restraining love is confirmed, human be- havior has a better chance to modify itself and conform to expectations. Once conformity is reached cohesive homeostasis in relations emerges. Attention from parents or authority figures can be interpreted as love, and as we well know, any attention is better than no attention at all. Yes, negative attention is better than none; at least the children know that parents take notice of them. That may well be the case with me and my siblings when we were children. Once we got our parents to come upstairs with that switch and they spanked us good, believe me we knew that total concentration was on us and then we went to sleep without any further annoyances. Maybe due to the less than romantic drama played out before us as kids, we interpreted one component of love as physical chastisement. Maybe sub- consciously we just wanted attention; I don't know, I'm not a physiatrist. That's just the way it went down!

While there are real issues that individuals face that need professional services, in many instances acting out can be no more complicated than one needing to understand that they have your love and acknowledgement. There are also cases of overkill when it comes to administering discipline. There are real incidents of abuse which must not and cannot continue. There must be balance in this area, as well as in all other aspects of relationships between individuals, especially between youths and adults. While caning may be a form of corporal punishment and may be described as overkill, this type of correction is akin to holding the reigns of the bit in a horse's mouth which controls and guides him.

I remember receiving four swats for not attending class in high school. I was found hanging out in the hall with some other students between classes. For the swat session, I was taken into the assistant principal's office and given a sound talking to about why it's important to be in class and on time and how I'm only hurting myself when I am in violation of school policy. Wow, that sounded so familiar; whenever mom or dad chastised me they said almost the same thing: *"I know you know better than doing that, this hurts me more than it does you, but you brought this on yourself,"* they would say.

After Mrs. Key gave me her entire spiel, she asked me to grab my ankles then the paddling commenced! Whack! The first swat rang out. My butt was toasty and warm after that sharp assault on my behind, but I was OK at this point. Whack, swat two! You know there is something about that second swat that is entirely unique. The first one warms you up but the second one is like a gauge which allows you to determine how you will fare through the entire swat session. If you take the second one OK, then the following swats are more likely to be OK as well. Somehow after number two I figured that I could make it. Swats three and four were like number two. Now mind you they did hurt; it hurt badly and I didn't want any part of that again. Mrs. Key, the assistant principal, was an average size woman and she hit me hard. However, there was a girl that I liked working as a student office helper that day. Her name was Carmen. Now Carmen, I really did like her, a lot! I had called her on the phone a few times and thought of her often away from school. My hope was that someday she would be my girlfriend. I'm sure she and everyone else in the outer office could hear what was going on inside where Mrs. Key and I were.

Well, needless to say, I was mortified by the actual swatting, but more so since Carmen my friend was aware of it. Although it hurt and I learned my lesson, the fact that my intended sweetheart and all the others in the office that day knew about the swatting I received, hurt worse. They knew I was getting a paddling. As I exited the inner office into the main outer office area, all eyes were on me, or at least it felt like they were. Before

I made it out of the main office door into the hall the tears began to flow. The humiliation was just too great for me to endure. That was the peer pressure component kicking in to finish the job. I didn't skip class again!

I think that we can learn a lot from these two situations, Fay's and mine. There is a wise saying which comes from the pages of the instruction Manual which reads as follows: *"Foolishness is bound up in the heart of a child, but the rod of correction drives it far from him; moreover, he will chastise his own sons and daughters because he loves them."* (Proverbs 22:15-16) Providing youth with chastisement or corrective measures teaches the "humility-ability paradigm," which is the capacity to look humbly at one's self and to treat others respectfully.

Remember when you were disciplined as a child and your mother, or whoever administered your punishment, spoke to you? Between sobs you answered, *"Yes ma'am" or "Yes sir."* That respectfulness jumped up in you and you realized that you were not the be all and end all. We have allowed public opinion and peer pressure to cause us to refrain from acts of real love toward our youth in the form of chastisement or correction. If we truly love, we put on the right path those our love is directed toward. We restrain them from taking the wrong path or lovingly guide them back onto the right path. Public opinion and political correctness are more aligned with mob mentality or group-think behavior than with individual choice. We must choose to care for our children or community by using the hearts and minds God gave us. There is a recognizable result that societies must deal with when we refuse to correct our youth.

In the Book of First Samuel, Chapter Two, we can read about the misdeeds of Eli's two sons. In the absence of correction by their father for their mischief, the entire family was disapproved.

Have you ever believed that a loved one, or anybody that you know for that matter, didn't care about you or for some reason didn't like you? If so, your reaction to their disapproval of you was most likely one of distancing yourself from them. Perhaps you said to yourself, *"Away with you then! I don't need you any way!"* That's kind of a way of saving face, as it were. We see this attitude in the demeanor of so many of today's youth. I believe it's a possible reaction that comes from not totally knowing, believing, or truly feeling the love and care needed and longed for from a progressively pleasure-hungry society focused on, *"Me, myself, and I."* If I were a visitor from another planet and I had to name the Earth based on the chief characteristic of its inhabitants, I would call it *"Memyselfand Island!"* Yes, that would be the appropriate name for Earth.

There are youths that do not receive proper love and concern from parents, parents who are otherwise occupied. Therefore, the peer pressure levied by youths who truly suspect that *"Their mommy or daddy does not care about them,"* impacts those who question if they are loved toward a more cynical view of their circumstances. This type of persuasion is subtle yet powerful. A statement from a peer such as, *"I don't care what my momma said, I'm going to the dance any way!"* When a youth that knows his or her parent is not actively engaged with them or really doesn't care too much what the child does, such a child may make a statement like that. But the influential sway that such a statement may have on a youthful mind which has to guess if his or her parents truly loves them can have negative consequences in the relationship between youths and their parents, especially after the enemy puts his manipulative spin on it.

I believe this is one of the main avenues by which we produce large numbers of reluctant youth, namely via **BPE**: **Busy** parents, **Peer** pressure, and the **Enemies** spin. Sometimes young people look for not only affirmation, but also correction and guidance.

Sidebar: *I believe that this is what many young people say to themselves: "I want to know that you want what's best for me and you are going to see to it even against my present posture. I'm uncertain of what I want and I believe you should know what's better for me. I'm holding you responsible and account-able and hoping against all hope that you come through for me. I may not even believe in you but I sure want you to believe in yourself. And most of all I want you to believe in me. Love me, care about me, please!"*

We must love others enough to lovingly speak the truth to them and make all the necessary deposits into them, either through tough love or simplistic compassion. Either way, love is the key. We must provide what's needed when it's needed and in the proper dosage. Providing the necessary correction when needed does indeed create an atmosphere in which order is established and maintained. I do not mean control or domi-nance, just simply order, organization, and harmonious stability. Certainly, if you set your mind to it, you can devise many bridges for our youth to cross over to a more sustainable shore of possibilities. Here are just a few that I suggest as starting points:

Advocate

- Become and activist. Demand that media refrain from promoting and targeting youth with appalling programming.
- Demand appropriate games, music, television, and movies.
- Be an appropriate role model for your youth. This means all youth within your circle of involvement.
- Keep your word.
- Spend quality time with youth; also, un-quality time, just hanging out.

- Help youth develop areas of interest that appeals to them; this means proactively, constructively, and financially, remain engaged.
- Involve youth in local politics.
- As parents and adults, learn about industry, technology, and science side by side with youth.
- Share your experiences, strengths, and hopes in an honest and candid way, and give the youth the opportunity to do the same without becoming judgmental.
- Monitor, maintain, and give youth more reasons to not only love you but like you as well.
- Attention, Affection, Affirmation.

Civic and Community Programs

For some, these functions will feel uncomfortable for a while, but, just like wearing seatbelts, you will get use to them. Seatbelts came into law in 1968. It was found that countless lives could be saved by making this simple adjustment when riding in a motor vehicle. That law required all passenger vehicles to be fitted with passenger restraints in all positions where passengers could be seated. From the mid-80s through the mid-90s law enforcement began ticketing drivers for not wearing seatbelts. This was a safety measure intended to save lives. Now it feels foreign to ride in a vehicle without first strapping in. Similarly, in a few years, if these simple guidelines are adhered to on a wide enough level, countless lives can be saved, and walking closely with our youth will feel like second nature just as wearing a safety belt feels normal today.

Organizations that provide unity, focus, and accomplishment are of upmost value to youth and the communities in which they live and serve. Below is a sampling of just a few such organizations, but I'm sure that many exist in your area that you may find beneficial to your young people.

Agents of Change (AOC), which began in 2003, brings delegations of U.S.-based youth to conferences and summits related to international sustainability policy, primarily at the United Nations. Young delegates work with government delegates, fellow civil society members, and other youth to promote cooperation, focusing on youth-friendly and future-oriented policies.

The Boy Scouts of America (BSA) is one of the largest youth organizations in the United States, with over four million youth members in its age-related divisions. Since its founding in 1907 as part of the international Scout Movement, more than 110 million Americans have been members.

The BSA's goal is to train youth in responsible citizenship, character development, and self-reliance through participation in a wide range of outdoor activities, educational programs, and, at older age levels, career-oriented programs in partnership with community organizations.

Boys & Girls Clubs of America (BGCA) is a national organization whose mission is to "enable all young people, especially those who need us most, to reach their full potential as productive, caring, responsible citizens."

Hip Hop 4 Life (Formerly Hip Hop 4 Health) is a not-for-profit youth empowerment organization dedicated to engaging, educating and empowering young people to adopt a healthy lifestyle. Health professionals, entertainers, celebrities and athletes are enlisted to educate young people on health issues through interactive workshops and empowerment seminars. Hip Hop 4 Life serves young people ages 10 through 18 years of age, with a special emphasis on at risk and low income youth.

Junior Achievement is a non-profit youth organization founded in 1919 by Horace Moses, Theodore Vail, and the late

Senator Winthrop M. Crane. This organization focuses on educating youth about the free enterprise system. Junior Achievement began on the East Coast of America as a collection of small, after-school business clubs for students. In 2004 the U.S. and international operations merged. Today Junior Achievement reaches nine million young people in 123 countries.

The National Youth Leadership Council, or **NYLC,** is a national nonprofit organization located in Saint Paul, Minnesota. The NYLC promotes service-learning in schools and communities across the United States. NYLC was founded in 1983 by James "Jim" Kielsmeier, who is the President and CEO. The NYLC sponsors the annual National Service-Learning Conference, which is designed to promote service-learning and national service within the United States.

Students Against Destructive Decisions (SADD) is a peer-to-peer youth education organization, focused on substance and alcohol use and abuse prevention. The organization has over 10,000 chapters in middle schools, high schools, and colleges in the United States and New Zealand.

SADD was founded in 1981 as "Students Against Driving Drunk" (occasionally and incorrectly called Students Against Drunk Driving) at Wayland High School located in Wayland, Massachusetts. This organization was formed after two Wayland High School hockey players were killed in separate car crashes. The students were motivated to challenge the culture in which drinking and driving was accepted.

Originally, SADD's mission was to help young people say *"No"* to drinking and driving, and to cocaine consumption. In 1997, SADD extended its mission from preventing intoxicated driving to preventing the consumption of alcohol or illegal drugs and other challenges. SADD now highlights prevention of all destructive behaviors and attitudes that are harmful to young people, including underage drinking, substance abuse, impaired driving, violence, and suicide.

After researching many youth programs I found that **Youth Excellence Performance Arts Workshop, or YEPAW**, was in my opinion one of the foremost and best current youth programs available. There are a myriad of other programs in which youth could become involved. The above organizations represent just a few of many groups in which youth can explore their potential and grow to reach their dreams.

I was fortunate enough to sit down with the founder of YEPAW, Mrs. Leslie Parker Barnes. She is the founder and Executive Director of YEPAW Youth Excellence Performance Arts Workshop. Responding to a comment made in 1990 regarding our youth as a "lost generation," Mrs. Barnes cried out, *"Not so!"* and promptly began to gather young people together. A gifted contralto, she resorted to what she knew well and loved passionately — music!

She invited some 50 young people to spend several hours a week with her. During those evenings, Mrs. Barnes taught the youth 10 songs in four-part harmony to be presented in a concert at the end of the week. She also solicited the help of local politicians, educators, medical professionals and business leaders to share their own personal stories of the triumphs and tragedies encountered on their journey to personal and professional success. She stressed courtesy, attention to detail, focus and determination. Individual talent was also acknowledged, but collective work and excellence were revered.

The success of the concert performed for parents and the community was its own reward. In 1993, Mrs. Barnes, a woman of faith, shared her dream of expanding and providing more opportunities for young people to pursue excellence through what was a less threatening venue for many — the performing arts. Often students do not experience great success in academic settings; therefore, every effort was made to show the correlation between effort and outcome. Commitment, practice, collaboration, refinement, and a willingness to expect and accept no less than the best in your craft was a transferable skill. Simply put, if you could produce a well-written poem, learn sign language, perform a drama, or learn complicated dance steps in just one week, then a similar application to school, home, and friends, could and would produce comparable results.

With the help and encouragement from a few "faithful" friends, the unwavering support of parents and other volunteers, assistance from the Akron faith community, business and nonprofit organizations, and collaboration with faculty and administration from The University of Akron, Mrs. Barnes' labor of love grew into an international phenomenon. Since 2001, the YEPAW experience has expanded to Cape Town and Durban, South Africa, with a taskforce exploring other venues in Africa and Europe. July 2017 marked 24 years of encouraging youth to pursue lifestyles of excellence!

Mrs. Barnes, a vibrant, witty, and pleasant person with an easy smile always at the ready, shared some of her very insightful ideas regarding youth with me. She said, *"I have worked with youth from the time I was too old to claim that I was a youth. I taught Sunday school as a young person; I taught music to young people ever since high school.*

"I have always been involved with young people. I work better with teenagers from the age of about twelve years old and up through twenty one-ish. I don't do too well with two and three year olds. My overall impression of today's youth is that they are living in some very tough times; they are going to have to make

some very hard choices. However, they cannot think that they are going to have a very good life and not have a good education. At least bottom line, a good skill, especially African American kids.

"It is not the lottery and it's not being discovered by a sports team or a record label necessarily, but all those things are possible. But as a young person it's going to be investing in myself to be a disciplined individual, everyday pouring into myself. They must live a quality life not so much having things, but they must have a purpose and planned life. Casual living just is not a good thing anymore because job markets are very small and employers are very particular about who they are going to hire. Opportunities are out there but you have to go after the opportunities. They are not coming to you!

"The most formidable challenge that young people face today, I think, is the amount of information they can get; information does not necessarily mean truth. What they get on television, facebook and online; they get all that information all the time. Without maybe the ability to decipher truth in it, it's just information and so they take on a lot of the lifestyles seen as if it's appropriate, and it is just not appropriate. Being able to disseminate maybe what I should take on and what I should run from; what I should embrace and what I should think of as taboo. I think that is their biggest challenge, being able to make a clean, clear choice."

Mrs. Barnes went on to say, *"Many of our young people feel that there is nothing they are unable to do. We are living in the era where Obama is President, and you know people use to say that an African American could rise to the highest office. Now they can see it and it is so possible; there really is nothing impossible if they put their minds to it. If they work as if they are planning for future success, there is nothing they cannot* accomplish. The scary thing is that maybe they think that it's going to be given to them and they won't have to work for it, and that's just not real."

She further stated that, "I think our kids still look for the examples and leadership and input from adults though. Really, yes, I really do believe that. I think they hunger for people they can look at who are walking what they talk. I think our kids long for adults who will stand beside them who are solid and walk in integrity. I think adults are so busy doing their own thing. Some of our adults are going back and reliving their childhood because they were so grown up too quickly. Now they have stepped back and are trying to relive things that they missed out on when they should have maybe gotten when they were teenagers.

"Now they don't have time for our kids. I think adults are so busy trying to make it for themselves that they forget that there is a generation that's learning. So, are we teaching them to be caring or are we teaching them to be selfish and it's all about "me?" We should be teaching them that I can get mine and enough for three or four other people. We should at least leave breadcrumbs so that at the end of the day people can say 'I followed her or I followed him. He taught me discipline, how to laugh, how to eat well, how to take care of my body or just general things.' These are the things that we have to leave for our children.

"As for the schools, our schools do what they can to provide knowledge and information. They cannot provide the passion. I think that is something the family or community does. They can provide the tools to the facility and people who care, but that is just a small portion of our children's education. We cannot think that the schools can teach our children the things that only a daddy can teach his son and what only a mommy can teach her daughter.

"The church, on the other hand, is a different animal alto-gether because the church gives me knowledge and it puts me in a position to hear calling and purpose. The church also gives me strength. In addition, it helps me understand who I am and why I am here; it affirms me and builds me. The church can be there for me in the nighttime and in the midday, my birthday, and my wedding. It participates in my whole life. So the church is a different animal altogether. Sure, it teaches me and trains me; it lifts me and feeds me. I think the church touches every part of my being.

"Now home life is crucial. Home should be the one place I can return to every day and feel safe. Feel like its OK to be me. Feel like it is OK if I'm silly or broken. The home is a lot of different places. Home may not be where mommy and daddy, sister and brothers are. Home may be where college students finally find their place on campus; where they feel safe. When they get back to their dorm room, they feel safe because in the home of origin, it was hell. And so that was a house and not necessarily a home and now they have found a place where they feel safe and secure; a place where they are growing and maturing. When they get back to the dorm and they lay their head down, that is a safe place, that's home.

"Yes, the home is crucial! Everybody needs a place where they can rest; a place where they can be at peace and feel affirmed and safe. It is different for different people, but let me be honest as to what I think your real question is. I think the home is necessary and we need to protect it because very many of our children don't have that. They don't have it where they can walk into their room, or come home and eat, or walk into the home and smell mom's food cooking. I grew up in a situation that when I walked into the house you could smell a pot of greens or maybe mom was baking cookies. Those things made you know that you were home. Just lying on the living room floor; that was my house and I knew that! I had ownership because this is where I lived. Everybody needs a home!

"We live in a great community here in Akron. You know people say that kind of stuff all the time, but this is an amazing community. When I think about the opportunities that I have had living right here, I have travelled the world and there is more of the world I want to see, but I will always come home. There is something about this community that is very unique. You could probably get an audience with the mayor; you can go in and talk with your council member; and you can call Marco (City Council President) on the phone. I think the community does try, but they are only human too, so they are not perfect. I'm sure they all have their agendas, but I think we live in a community that is trying to help its youth. They are trying to provide programming for youth, such as Project Grad. Also, I could not do YEPAW if it were not for this community. Community leaders have supported us with funding and they come in often to talk to our kids, volunteering and spending time with us. We put these people in office and we should hold them accountable to be and do all they said they would do."

I asked Mrs. Barnes about the hip-hop (also called rap music) revolution, and she provided the following:

"Hip-hop? My greatest concern about hip-hop? Well let me be positive first: it's creative. Kids love it and it's hard not to move your body when hip-hop is being played and not bounce because it's just a powerful medium. So I am not mad at that. I'm not necessarily a fan of hip-hop though. Hip-hop is not my favorite type of music, but neither is country and western for that matter. But some of the messages (with strong emphasis she said), especially against women, that have become accepted, and when I hear some of our young people use the language, not necessarily just the foul language, cursing, and all that kind of stuff, that's just crude in and of itself. Why would I sit and listen to that kind of stuff? To me that kind of talk is just an uneducated, ignorant person having a very limited vocabulary. If that is the only way to show me that you're angry or make your point, that's sad. But when it speaks about women in such a derogatory way and we consider that entertainment, I think it's detestable!

"And it burdens me when I see young girls embrace that as if that's who I have to be, or that it's OK for someone to describe me like that, and for me to think that's an affectionate term. And the T-shirts that dudes wear called a wife beater; so now when I put that shirt on am I a wife beater? Is that OK? No! But it's cool or it's alright. It's like I'm talking affectionately that he will put that on with the potential that he might knock me down. Oh my God! That's my greatest concern about hip-hop. It speaks often, not all the time, but too often it tears down women. Where would we be without strong confident women who stood anyway? Who bore under the heat after having actually been beaten, came home and loved their children and cooked for their families? And how dare we, with that kind of rich heritage of what we have stood up under, make our young girls think someone can speak to them in that way and it's appropriate! That's my concern!

"Young boys who I know are good boys, feel the need to drupe their pants. My son is a good guy and even now I have to say to him 'Pull your pants up' or 'Where's your belt?' Why is it that this has infiltrated so into our culture? You will see grown men walking around like that you know, and I tell them all the time, 'I have a husband and a son; I don't need to see your underwear; I see enough underwear.' Very seldom in the music videos do we see the men scantily dressed, but the women have on next to nothing? To me that screams that there is an imbalance. I'm not telling the men to take their clothes off; I'm saying to the women, 'Put some on!'"

Consistent with what Mrs. Barnes is saying, I have noticed that some women have blouses down to the lowest possible point of the neckline. The bigger the breast the more willing the possessor of them seems to be inclined to bare them in public, and I must admit that as a man, it's not always very easy to look away quickly.

While too often women sport low, cleavage barring necklines, on most men's shirts the necklines fit around the neck as if a chokehold is being applied. Albeit the message is subtle, it's powerful and progressive. The dresses and the short shorts get shorter and the cleavage gets more and more noticeable. It's as if it's hidden, but in plain sight. *"That is just how it is,"* is what they will tell you. Its today's style!

We create a portrayal for our youth of a world where public nudity, indecency and pornography are just another pursuit in life. Women are just objects and there are no consequences or moral implications for anything. Maybe I am O.F. (old-fashioned) because I do not understand why this is so. Why do so many play this game, or get played by this game, is a more accurate question? To me personally, it seems that a woman having a very seductive and alluring part of her anatomy would reserve it for the special man in her life, not anybody within eyeshot. Moreover, why do I as a public citizen have to be subjected to viewing women's naked bodies if I do not wish too at that time? Just because I am at the mall looking for a new pair of shoes, I must also look at your boobs too, right? I admire the female form just like any normal man; boobs are great, don't get me wrong. Why can't I pick the time and place and whose boobs I want to look at? Just because I'm downtown on a warm summer day, I must force myself to quiet my hormones because you feel the need to uncover yourself in public, right? Most embarrassingly for us as a culture, when I go to church to receive strength and empowerment for the trials that lay ahead, I have to force my eyes away from ample bosoms bubbling over the top of your low-cut blouse, right? Other than my own wife's uncovered body, who else should I be looking at? Again, I must be out of touch with the now, or maybe I am just O.F.

Mrs. Barnes went on to say, *"In the hip-hop medium women have become no different from a chair or the wall; they are just an object to sell the music."*

"As for the drug culture in present day society I'll say this, it's tough because we live in such a materialistic world, the 'get it quick age.' I'm supposed to push a button and make it happen. You remember we used to have to walk across the room to change the TV channel? 'Get out of here!'" Mrs. Barnes and I shared a laugh at this nostalgic reminiscence: *"People today would think how barbaric that is. Kids don't even think or understand the idea of hard work, but yet in a way they do. Standing out there in the rain, looking for the police, checking over your shoulder to make sure somebody is not going to try and jump you for the money or the dope you got; that's not easy; that's a very dangerous life. You can make a lot of money but you can lose your life. The risks that you take! All of that brain work, it takes to do all of that. All of the weighing out of the drugs and separating it out, you could get an honest job or make your own job with those skills. These kids are smart. We could stop drugs from coming into this country but the people in power are making money on it. They could open the border up tomorrow and be giving crack away, but if we the people said 'Not in my neighborhood!' That's how we stop it.*

"As far as mainstream media, some of these commercials are very offensive. There is this Burger King commercial where they talk about square butts; it's very offensive. It's all about making quality decisions. Anything you want to see or view, it's either online or on TV or videos. You know that our eyes are the portal

to our core being. Why be delivered from all that stuff when it's just common sense to know that just because something is available doesn't mean that I have to participate in it or look at it.

"You know another thing that disturbs me is that it seems that somebody came in and changed the price tag and made the family cheap. You hear young girls say things like 'Oh he's so cute, I want to have his baby, or I love him so much I want to have his baby.' Girls having babies and throwing big baby showers and such has become all too common. We need to teach our girls to value themselves; terminology that we just accept today is just frightening to me. All of us have made mistakes and gotten into situations, so this is not an indictment on anyone who has had a child out of wedlock. We are raising a generation who are seeing this as the accepted way to go. We need to make decisions to have a quality life, and like I always say, this is not a hopeless generation."

Quality living and quality choices, as Mrs. Barnes puts it, are a must for us right now if we are to forward to the next generation the ability to possess a greater quality of life. As community, religious, education, business and family leaders of the present day, let us lead circumspectly with all prudence because the legacy we leave behind us has far, far reaching implications for the wellbeing of humankind and the Earth upon which we all live.

We must dare to dream, just as Dr. Martin Luther King, Jr. dreamed and explored the possibilities of true righteousness and take the initiative to grow towards it.

Somewhere there must be a place in our hearts and minds that lead us into realities that we have not at present fully developed. Altruistic moral fiber is a necessary component which leads us toward the fertile heritage we were predestined to attain as human beings.

The Wizard Of Oz!

In the movie *The Wizard of Oz*, Dorothy, played by Judy Garland, sings about a land she dreams of one day reaching. She says something very interesting before she begins the song. When Auntie Em tells her to go someplace where she won't get into any trouble Dorothy says, *"Someplace where there isn't any trouble, do you suppose there is such a place, Toto? There must be. It's not a place you can get to by a boat or a train, but it's far, far away behind the moon, beyond the rain."* Then she sings the words to this very hopeful and inspiring song declaring: *"Somewhere over the rainbow, way up high."* Dorothy recounts what she has heard about and sings on: *"There's a land that I heard of, once in a lullaby."*

Dorothy relies on faith and believes that her dreams can come true. When she sings in her beautiful alto voice, *"Somewhere over the rainbow, skies are blue, and the dreams that you dare to dream, really do come true."* Dorothy knows that if it can be done, she too, could possess the things she dreams of most as she emphatically implored: *"If happy little bluebirds fly, beyond the rainbow, why, oh why can't I?"*

We can hear so much of what we should demand of life in the words of this prayer. Yes, it is somewhat of a prayer; it is a prayer that indicates that the place we currently find ourselves is not our end of the line. From here we strive to apprehend our hopes and dreams, not only by wishing for them, but by putting forth effort. We must never submit to the demand of our present circumstances to quit. On the contrary, we compel our circumstance to give way to our inner strength and fortitude, self-determination, and Godly grit! We are in the driver's seat of destiny. We decide our own famine or fortune. If unfavorable circumstances currently exist in our lives, we have the right and the authority to keep such circumstances as they exist, change, or to expel them.

What is more, the story of *The Wizard of Oz* shares with us insights into what each of us could lay hold of if we are honest with ourselves. If we take a true self-inventory and challenge the places of weakness or deficiencies within, we too, can fly above the rainbows of life. If we dared to dream and truly believe that our visualizations could come to pass, what bold, affirmative progress we could make! We could build momentum for ourselves and the generations following. All Dorothy wanted was to get back home to her family that loved and cared for her, and to feel the warmth of the land and the care to which she had become accustomed.

The Scarecrow felt that he was not witty or intelligent because he had no brain. Dorothy asked him what he would do if he did have a brain. He sang out his self-affirming announcement of what he would hope to do. He said, for example, his *"Head he would be scratchin, while his thoughts were busy hatchin, if he only had a brain."* He further went on to say that, *"I'd unravel every riddle for any individual, in trouble or in pain. And with the thoughts I'd be thinkin, I could be another Lincoln, if I only brain."* The Scarecrow, all stuffed with hay and covered in patchwork, dared to allow his inner self to express the deepest longings he had buried deep inside, and what he planned to do after his dream had come true.

All the travelers along the yellow brick road stood and faced their fears and the longstanding strongholds that were present in their lives. They chose to believe that there was one who could bring closure to the chapter in their lives where lack and oppression ruled. They dared to trust that there was one who possessed the power and ability to provide what they lacked, or that which they thought they lacked.

Even the Tin Man, suffering the lack of a heart, believed that he could not love or be loved because he didn't have a heart. He said the tin smith forgot to give him a heart. *"No heart,"* the others said in unison? *"No heart, all hollow,"* he replied. He acknowledged that he was all tin and hollow, yet he dared to dream of what being complete and whole would be like. He sang and danced very animated as he visualized joyfully what being made complete would bring to his life. He said, *"When a man's an empty kettle, he should be on his mettle, and yet I'm torn apart. Just because I'm presumin' that I could be kind-a-human, if I only had heart."*

Saddest of all is the Cowardly Lion, born to rule the forest, to be "King of the jungle," and "King of the beasts," and to have dominion over all that he surveyed (just like you and I). But he was so afraid that his own shadow caused him to go into hiding. How similar he is to so many of us. We were given dominion in the garden, only to relinquish our authority to a crafty creature. The Lord has restored us, yet we remain timid. Dorothy confronted the Cowardly Lion and called him a coward. He agreed with her assessment of him and repeated what she called him out of his own mouth: *"You're right, I am a coward,"* he said. How many times do others call us what we are not created to be, and we voice our agreement with their assessment of us?

Our Creator says that we are more than conquerors through His love, yet we don't really stand in the light of that truth. *"I haven't any courage at all"* the Cowardly Lion said. And during his self-evaluation he said something that almost knocked me off my seat. He said, *"It's been in me so long I just had to tell you how I feel."* How many of us have longstanding strongholds that have held us back for so long? It's time to get it off your chest! There are family strongholds that have been so longstanding that they have become camouflaged. That's just the way it is in the family and no one knows why and doesn't much care anymore.

The Cowardly Lion sang out that he could, *"Show his prowess, be a lion not a mouess, if he only had the nerve."* Suddenly there was unity and comradery among the yellow brick road travelers! They were all on one accord, seeking what they felt they didn't have. I believe many of today's youth gangs begin in similar fashion: a comradeship forms among individuals seeking that which they feel they lack. As the drama continues the hopeful foursome arrives in the inner sanctum of the Wizard, from whom they desire to receive that which they believe they sorely lack.

In my view, what happens upon their entrance, before the perceived might of the known world could be labeled as a metaphor for some of our life circumstances today. How they boast against us, attempting to bring us under subjection to whatever difficulties they present in our lives.

Smoke flashing, threatening visual images, thunderous explosive booms, all which give entrance to the figure of an individual of frightening proportions. His visage angry and confident, his words are callus and rough. This individual then rises above the four quivering seekers and boastfully declares in a hostile, aggressive manner, *"I am Oz, the great and powerful! Who are you?"* Mind you, if you have ever seen or read the story of *The Wizard of Oz*, you know it's just a little old man behind a curtain pulling levers and amplifying his voice to create illusionary perceptions of his dominance, power and greatness.

This charlatan is very much like the con artist that usurps authority over much of our life circumstances, placing us on the defensive, boasting of his greatness, creating images and illusion, not realities. Eventually, as the story unfolds, this fraud admitted that everything each of them wanted, they already possessed; they simply had to receive affirmation. The very things that they needed or felt deprived of was in their possession all the time. It was all smoke and mirrors all along; not just on the Wizard's home court, but from times long past the feelings of deprivation, fear, isolation, and inferiority were just delusions, apparitions, and phantoms. Affirmation, love and approval would win out.

Many times, we chase these ghosts all of our lives and come to the end of our road — yellow brick or not — only to find that what we thought we needed was extraordinarily unimportant or it was something we already possessed, just labeled under a different file title. You can open your own mouth and use your own tongue and declare *"Be gone!"* to the things that you need to move out of your way, proclaim, *"Off with your heads"* to fear and doubt when they attempt to hinder your progress; *"Off with your heads"* to generational curses and family dysfunction; *"Off with your heads"* when obstacles and foreboding mountains threaten your progress.

Sharing My Hope & Dreams!

All my life I wanted to have a peaceful life with the woman of my dreams; the woman who I loved and cared for, and she loved and cared for me right back. I wanted no financial worries, and just wanted to raise the children that are our crowning joy. I had it all figured out! This was my world and I was going to shape it to fit my vision; all was going to be just grand. Well, life has a way of throwing you a curve ball sometimes. As Forrest Gump put it, *"You never know what you're gonna get"* once you open the box.

I was then reacting to life as a spectator, not as an authoritative participant. We must live life with recognition of who and what we are. We must understand that circumstances are not our masters, they are simply a result of cause and effect. The engine that mobilizes our lives is our faith, and our desire is at the steering wheel.

I think most of the time people readjust their vision of life to fit the reality they find themselves in at a given point in time. A succession of readjustments, reassessment, and more readjustments — that's life! Clear goals and steps to reach those goals without losing sight of them are possible and necessary components to successful living. Just as clear goals and steps to reach those goals are absolutes, so is faith and trust that God will see us through to the end and prosper our vision if we truly trust in Him to do so.

Just about everybody has a concern about money at some point in their lives — if not all their lives! We work and save; make logical purchases with the intent that there will be a little money left when the smoke clears after high gas prices, bills, never ending needs of family life, taxes, and so on, have been paid. Somehow it seems that there is always more month left at the end of the money than money left at the end of the month, and the budget is constantly being readjusted. As for the "happy ever after" life with the person of your dreams — with no problems, always blissfully idyllic, delightful, joyful, with peace everlasting; "*Ha- Ha- Ha- Ha- Ha- Ha- Ha- Ha!*" Imagine that!

Healthy, happy, successful children, being the crowning joy of hard working, well intentioned parents, can be realized with cooperation by both parents and children. I know people who seem to have that equation worked out, and family life appears to be functioning like a well-oiled machine, working as it was planned, with happy kids and parents alike. However, we don't know what really goes on behind the closed doors of someone else's household. Apparently, well-functioning families have their difficulties too. It's in the daily grind of working out these problems in a loving and patient way that we develop teaching opportunities for all. We adults learn as well as our youth if we remain engaged, not allowing hardship to break the fellowship among us.

Some of us parents make mistakes, bringing about the undesired result of greater levels of family dysfunction. We cry, *"This is the way my daddy did it,"* or *"My momma always said this is the way things are done."* You know what they say, the grass always looks greener on the other side, but looks can be deceiving. What variable makes one family more functional than another? Is it genetics, opportunities, upbringing, exposure, quality time, love and caring? Yes! All the above and much, much more! I believe it is all worth every moment invested if the next generation is truly advanced beyond the level of this present age bracket of the 40 plus.

Advancement doesn't necessarily mean bigger, faster, or stronger. True advancement will stimulate cooperation, caring, service-oriented communities, reconciliation, and greater levels of harmonious living. Stay involved in your youth's growth and development. If you have not found an appropriate youth organization, be it faith, community, cultural or sporting based for your youth, find one! Do not simply send them, but become involved with them also. I'm sure you will be pleased with the experiences that your young person comes away with because of this activity.

Sidebar*: If you see a problem and the answer does not appear anyplace in sight, go to the mirror and you will find the answer. A problem without an answer only indicates that the answer is in you. Remember grade school when the teacher called on you and you had to produce the answer to a specific problem? Life is just like that! We all must answer when life calls on us. Too often we remain silent when we are called upon, resulting in a low mark, or we are retained. Give the correct answer next time you're called upon!*

Media & Entertainment!

Back in the day I loved to watch NBA and college basketball. I can remember watching some of the great players of yesteryear, such as Jo Jo White of the Boston Celtics, and Wilt Chamberlin as the highly touted center when he was with the Los Angeles Lakers. I even remember Robert "Chief" Parish coming into the league as a rookie! Wow! That's kind of back there, isn't it? How about Magic Johnson and Larry Bird playing college basketball, each at their respective universities?

I saw Willis Reed come out of the locker room to lead the Knicks to the championship over the Lakers in the 1970 finals. It was Game Seven, and nobody knew if Willis Reed would play. The center and captain of the New York Knicks had a torn muscle in his right thigh. He had injured it during Game Five against the Los Angeles Lakers, and had not played in Game Six when Wilt Chamberlain's 45 points and 27 rebounds enabled the Lakers to tie the series at 3-3.

When the teams took the floor for pre-game warm-ups, Reed was not on the floor with his New York teammates. He had remained in the locker room. Reed took an injection to slow the pain in his leg, and just moments before tipoff he limped through the tunnel and onto the court. Waves of cheers cascaded down from the Garden stands as fans caught the image of the Knicks' captain coming out onto the floor. Reed's presence was more than enough to inspire the Knicks to a victory and the franchise's first NBA Championship. Overshadowed by Reed's emotionally charged effort was one of the great playoff performances in NBA history by Walt Frazier, who led the Knicks with 36 points and 19 assists. What a game!

As for football, I enjoyed greats such as Buck Buchannan of the Kansas City Chiefs, and I saw Johnny Unitas and Bart Starr play. I remember Walter Payton and Gale Sayers, who had his short-lived career depicted in the movie *Brian's Song* starring Billy Dee Williams and James Caan. It was one of my all-time favorite movies. Some of the greatest games in my opinion were played in the archives of history past.

Here is the setup: On second down and 35 yards to go, Morton threw a pass; the pass went through the hands of running back Dan Reeves. It was intercepted by Colts linebacker, Mike Curtis, who returned the ball 13 yards to the Cowboy's 28 yard line. The Colts field goal kicker, O'Brien, kicked a successful 32-yard field goal, giving Baltimore a 16-13 lead with five seconds left in the game. That was a description of the last few minutes of Super Bowl V. What drama! What intrigue! I was so pumped as the ball went through the uprights for the win. What about the immaculate reception by Franco Harris? Wow! Such excitement, thrills, and enjoyment!

Not to discriminate by omitting some memorabilia for you women, Tom Selleck, star of *Magnum PI*, and Billy Dee Williams, had you thinking thoughts back in the day, didn't they? Come on, you can admit it. I won't tell anybody. The bathtub love scene in the movie *Super Fly* between leading actor Ron O'Neal, who played Youngblood Priest, and actress Sheila Frazier, who played Georgia, sparks one's imagination! It's hard not to think about things like that sometimes. I must admit, I imagined myself as *Super Fly* in that tub with that fine woman a time or two myself!

Sports figures and the exorbitant salaries they receive makes one want to play for a sports franchise. Mind you, I am all for people earning as much as they can. I am very happy to see folks make as much as they do on their jobs. No hate, appreciate! Contrast the millions made annually by entertainment industry figures, baseball, football or basketball players who truly do entertain and inspire us. But compare the money they make with the salaries received by our teachers, preachers, doctors, law enforcement officers, and sanitation service workers who perform the really needed services within the communities in which we live. It goes without saying, our youth are at least twice as likely to be impacted by the glamour and notoriety of the sports and entertainment world than a more attainable and common career choice which helps to sustain a community.

Remember, everybody wants to be loved? We indeed love our entertainers. To be ordinary is just that, ordinary, and we've taught our youth that they must be extraordinary to be somebody in this world. It's almost like choosing pop over water; the water is life sustaining and heath promoting but the soda-pop tastes better. Or, it's like choosing Barabbas over Christ. Christ is the one I need to be truly free, but Barabbas is an old friend. We're more familiar and comfortable with Barabbas. With him I don't have to do anything to change, or accept anything uncomfortable.

To change the way things have been forever takes time and determination. We seem to be timid in taking the necessary steps to have a better world personally and/or globally. We demand that which titillates and satiates our appetites. We clamor for what we can have right now. Our kids likewise are being taught by us to choose convenience, pleasure, or profit over integrity and value. It's not so much that we teach them this by what we say, but it's what they see daily. Not only from us as parents but across the nation and worldwide as well.

The soulful sounds of the *Motown* groups and its singers influenced the nation and even the world. *"Innnntroducing the tempting Teeeemptations!"* The music begins with the beat of the drum, then you hear the bass kick in, a little guitar, then the sweet organ sounds ring out. The backbeat is so catchy! The crowd is so hyped in anticipation of seeing the Temps; the atmosphere is so electric. Then David, Otis, Eddy, Paul, and Melvin burst on to the stage through the curtain. Oh, check out the steps! The harmony is so tight and the band is kickin! Wow, and that's my favorite song too! What a great performance. I think I'll buy their album on the way out. This was a great concert, wasn't it? Yea man, the Temptations were off the hook. Yup! A likely conversation that many concert goers might have had with their friends after attending such an event!

The Supremes, Marvin Gaye, The Jackson Five; whatever your favorite musical group, favorite sport or sports team, movie, or other form of entertainment, man oh man, what impact they had and continue to have on us as a nation and on us just as people individually! The music, the sporting events and the movies all contributed prominently in the chasing and catching of the girls, and the girls getting their guys. Either way, we spent hours, days and nights, which became weeks, just pursuing our fantasies! The weeks became months, and the months grew into years, and the years became lifetimes of being entertained.

Entertainment is defined as amusement or diversion, provided especially by performers, something diverting or engaging. Diversion is defined as the act or an instance of diverting from a course, activity, or use. It is something that diverts or amuses. It can also be described as a pastime. We all know that a diversion can be a temporary traffic detour. A diversion may also be defined as an attack, trick, or ploy that draws the attention and force of an opponent or enemy from the primary point of operation.

Can you wrap your head around that for a moment? Has an enemy diverted our attention from his primary point of operation while we smiled and sang along or cheered at the entertainment before us? Have we also been diverted away from our primary focus?

Sidebar: As a generation, nationwide and worldwide, have we stayed too long at the fair?

We immersed ourselves with phone conversations, TV screens, movie screens, or recreational parks. We were totally consumed by the icons or idols of the day. We tried on different personas based in part on what we heard or saw in these mediums. We also experimented with different partners, attempting to find the right fit for the persona we had assumed, based largely on the fictitious images we see and hear through the media. Once we found that special personality or person which fit just right with the facade we had settled on, we put them on like a suite of clothing and they became part of our identity. With them we bought homes, raised families, grew older, and subsequently looked back with fondness and nostalgia. In some cases, we look with regret as days spent long ago haunted us like a phantom as that dream of ours lingered yet unfulfilled. Yes, unfulfilled due to the caricature of an idol or inauthentic personality we present due in part or in whole because we had been duped by media falsehood.

It is amazing how we focus so much time, attention and money on things that bring zero productivity into our lives. Have we not ascertained any insights from those who have passed on before us who, having lived long, seemingly rich lives, only to come to the end of the line unfulfilled, unactualized, and defeated in life because of incomplete or unfulfilled purpose?

There is need for leisure, rest and relaxation in our daily lives. But too often the pursuit of such becomes the goal in life. Diversion can become the opiate of the masses when time and again it's pursued at all cost. I personally must admit that I have spent days in front of the TV during playoff time, watching game after game. In fact, the other day as I watched the Michigan State vs. Iowa football game where it was reported that 57,178 people were in attendance, I really took note of how the crowd reacted as the game progressed. As Michigan State appeared to be the obvious winner after having scored with only seconds left, the Iowa faithful held on, hoping for a last second miracle.

Iowa, now driving the ball down the field, first down after first down, and soon Iowa is down around the Michigan State goal line. Failing to get in for the touchdown on three consecutive attempts and on the very last play of the game with two seconds left on the clock, a touchdown is scored and Iowa wins. The crowd goes wild. Hands immediately go up together in true jubilation! Voices ring out with accolades and praise for the person or the play that scored the winning touchdown. Dancing and merriment commence. People who otherwise would never mingle are giving each other the "high fives," and even hugging.

Everyone knows what the symbols and calls mean in their sport of choice and are willing to pay large sums of money to be present at the games. We pay through the nose for the paraphernalia associated with the game, player or team we follow. The fact that we pay our sports figures millions of dollars per season to catch, punch, hit, drive, kick, run, block, tackle, throw and dunk for our amusement is very telling about our culture.

This all reminds me of what is described in the pages of the Manual as the early worshipers would gather to laud praise onto deities. On one accord hands and voices were raised and sacrifices were made. We say that we trust in God, we say that we believe only He can bring salvation to us. In contrast to how much time, energy and money we spend on our idols versus God, it seems the jury is still out regarding the claim that God is number one in our lives.

On Fridays, we have high school football. Saturdays, its college, and on Sundays there is pee wee and pro, which keeps the true fan busy for the weekend. During the week, we work and recuperate from the previous weekend's rout of our team and prepare for the games scheduled for the upcoming weekend. When football season ends we have basketball and then baseball. In between we have the Olympics, summer games, WWE wrestling and so on and so forth — ad infinitum.

Think about this for a minute: At the Super Bowl, there could be as many as 80,000 in attendance. Add to this crowd the teams, stadium workers, attendants, security, and media personnel. Then include the millions upon millions watching worldwide on TV, or the Internet, and the millions more who listen on the radio. Consider all the commercial advertising generating billions in revenue, the fanfare leading up to the game, and the paralysis of analysis beginning weeks before the game. With all this blossoming into an almost religious-like fervor by game day, we can then include the praise and worship leaders called cheerleaders, dancers, and the halftime guest soloist. Throw in the sacrifices everyone makes to attend the game and the Super Bowl parties nationwide. I believe you can see where I'm going with this. When we really stop to think about it you must admit it's kind of scary.

I love sports! I grew up playing and watching sports. Can you recite the batting average of your favorite player or the probability that this team will beat the other team? Who do you think will win the championship this year? In sports arenas, the thousands in attendance plus the millions watching on TV and Internet are all in accord at that particular time. They are all focused on how the team will fare today. As the Michigan State vs. Iowa game came closer to the final play the commentator said, *"It just doesn't get any bigger or better than this."* Sadly, for too many of us, that is all too true!

We settle for and are even happy with the average, when we are created to soar well above average; to fly on wings like that of the great eagle. Like the great Muhammad Ali spoken of earlier who refused to settle for mediocrity, we must also seek our destiny with fervor and diligence. We lose ourselves in misdirection plays and thus become vulnerable to being scored against in life when we just settle.

I watched my four-year-old grandson as he watched the television program *SpongeBob SquarePants*. I had prepared his lunch and allowed him to eat while looking at Patrick and Squidward play with SpongeBob in the imagination box. My grandson repeatedly would stop eating and just stare into the set, fixed on what he was seeing, almost like a deer caught in the spotlight of a hunter. In a way, that is a more accurate depiction than it is an inaccurate one.

I spoke to him a couple of times about finishing his meal and I honestly believe he didn't hear me. It seems that we likewise put our awareness of most principal things on hold and stare into a fantasy world of entertainment for large chunks of our lives. We spend so much of our energy, time, and money on that which has a negative net return ratio. Parishioners peruse with vigor and have fixation on such pastime activities as much as individuals who do not claim piety or faith in anything sacred as well. And there is nothing wrong with these pastime activities. I still love and participate as well as watch many forms of sporting activities and other entertainment. However, I must admit it's very easy to become absorbed by them.

As a man of faith however, I ask myself why so many prayers seemingly go unanswered and why so much tribulation seems to dance merrily unabated in the lives of so many believers, including mine. While there is nothing iniquitous or naughty inherent in most entertainment, my submission to diversion can allow me to be taken captive, fostering an idol worship of sorts. When I become immersed in that which takes hold of me and ushers me away from truth or that which produces Godly profit, I error.

Idol worship is the belief that anything besides God can help us, or if I hold something as essential as, or more important than, God, I enter a forbidden zone of sorts. For example, if I view my property as more significant or more important than God, then I error. If I give my job as much or more time and attention than I give to God, or if I spend more time wondering where Lebron is going to play next year and become more emotionally tied to his decision than I do to the things of God — I am committing idol worship.

Sometimes we sit in church praying. But how often are we praying that the preacher would hurry up and finish so we can zip home because the game is coming on today? Consider the time we spend daily, how much of that time is utilized in the performance of seeking God or carrying out His will or commands? What percentage of our time do we utilize fulfilling our true purpose compared to the time we spend viewing some form of entertainment?

Unfortunately, I would suppose the clear majority of people who believe in God commit this gross offense of idol worship without even realizing it. How much of our day is spent on TV, idle talk, gossip, news, other people, our car, lawn, home maintenance, shopping, telephone, Internet, work, sleep, entertainment, and so on, vs. Godly endeavors? Take an inventory of your own life and see how you spend your time, talent, and money. This has tremendous and far reaching implications on future generations. Pay special attention to the following paragraph and note what is implied for future generations:

In Exodus 20:3-6 of the Manual we find the following commandment: *"Thou shall have no other gods before me. Thou shall not make unto thee any graven image, or any likeness of anything that is in heaven above, or that is in the earth beneath, or that is in the water under the earth. Thou shall not bow down thyself to them, nor serve them: for I the Lord thy God am a jealous God, visiting the iniquity of the fathers upon the children unto the third and fourth generation of them that hate me; And showing mercy unto thousands of them that love me, and keep my commandments."*

It may be difficult for us to see ourselves as practicing or participating in such activity as idol worship, however there is so much recreational activity these days that it is very challenging to perceive clearly that which may or may not be false and misleading. The word "recreation" itself, is obviously a compound word formed from "re," meaning to do again, and "creation," which is the act of creating. In its simplest form, creation is the act of making, inventing, or producing. From a biblical perspective creation is the act of bringing the world into ordered existence.

We can deduce that, while in recreation mode, we remake or reshape our world; we enter the domain of fantasy or imagination. Is that an unhealthy practice in which to engage? How we train our offspring is what I am currently focusing on.

We are rapidly heading toward the culmination of Christ's return. As we move swiftly into the future, the fashion in which we finish is of paramount importance. There is a reality that we must be prepared to deal with now and in the future if we are to survive as a human race. Remember, we are one people created by God and the longstanding premise that we have been on a journey here on Earth remains viable today. From ancient times through eternity we must travel this path as one race, the human race! Is it good enough to remain focused on the left when our destiny is to the right?

I have heard the statement, *"You better get right or you'll get left."* What does that statement sound like it is saying to you? As a culture, we have provided youth with diversions for many decades. Generation after generation we divert our attention from the reality of who we are and what we are doing or should be doing here on Earth. Presently the entertainment world feeds our youth with a steady pipeline of filth and misdirection. The hook is firmly in place in a manner of speaking and now anything coming down the pipe is fed unabated to us as adults as well as to our youth. Sadly, we have come down to even watching poker on the sports network. Yes, poker as a spectator sport! POKER! Really, POKER! My how the mighty have fallen! Industry moguls make every effort to create images that capture the imagination of our youth, and as we are all aware, the body and the money go where the head goes.

"Free your mind and your ass will follow!" — George Clinton

The Manual says that we are to transform ourselves by the renewing of our minds. It's time to restore our hearts and minds to the liberty we have been called to by the ALMIGHTY through Christ who is the transformative word of God. What we ingest through our eyes and ears can be either helpful or harmful, just as the types of foods we put into our bodies can benefit or destroy.

Food 4 Thought

Just as food nourishes our bodies and provides energy for us to grow and work, some foods can be disease-causing and bring our bodies into a less centered homeostasis. Like every other area of our society, we as adults produce and distribute the consumables that our youth feed upon. We are responsible for our young receiving healthy diets or poor ones. Akida J. Green, M.D., of Lake West Hospital in Willoughby, Ohio, provided the following helpful information in a personal interview:

*"**Pop or Soda:** This is known to increase the likelihood of obesity, osteoporosis, diabetes mellitus, coronary artery disease,*

tooth decay, and hypertension. The amount of sugar in one serving of soda is about 100% of the RDA! There are absolutely no nutritional benefits to taking in pop or soda, whether traditional pop or 'diet' pop, which tends to have aspartame, which is linked to headaches, worsening depression, increased hunger; links to cancers and aspartame is still being aggressively investigated.

*"**Chips:** The main negative effects of chips are salt and the fact that it is fried, which means it is high in saturated fat. Chips vary in their negative effects, so it's not fair to group them all in the same class. For example, comparing a typical 'potato chip' with say a whole grain chip (such as Sun Chips), you can expect entirely different profiles.*

*"**Fast food:** I can testify directly that fast food is an evil. In my second year of medical school, I gained 30 pounds in about nine months because of sedentary lifestyle combined with daily fast food consumption! Fast food is very high in calories compared to fresh foods (about 1,000 calories on average per meal, twice the average non fast food meal), it is also high in saturated fats, and generally, increases one's risk of atherosclerotic heart disease. Finally, it is well documented that fast food has harmful additives that decrease colonic activity, increasing one's likelihood for gastrointestinal syndromes (constipation, etc).*

*"**Tobacco:** Tobacco use has been directly linked to multiple cancers (lung, pancreas, oral, etc) cardiovascular disease (heart attacks and strokes), peptic ulcer disease (stomach ulcers), osteoporosis, and of course, chronic respiratory problems (emphysema/COPD, chronic bronchitis). It is the number one cause of preventable death in the United States. The only known benefits of tobacco consumption that I am aware of are appetite suppression and symptomatic relief of ulcerative colitis (although one's risk of colon cancer would thus be increased in a patient with ulcerative colitis who concomitantly smoked tobacco).*

Finally, tobacco is highly addictive, and one of the most difficult drugs to come off of.

"**Alcohol consumption:** Alcohol is also highly addictive. It has been directly linked to multiple cancers (liver cancer, oral-/esophageal cancers), liver failure (cirrhosis), dementia, peripheral neuropathy, birth defects, gastritis (stomach inflammation and bleeding), gastrointestinal bleeding (varices, hemorrhoids, etc.), blood dyscrasias (splenomegaly/thrombocytopenia, etc.), respiratory depression (coma or death in excess), and is one of the few drugs that can lead to death upon rapid cessation (delirium tremens). Alcohol is one of the few things on this list that has beneficial effects if used in moderation, i.e., (one, five ounce glass of red wine per day for women, or 10 ounces for men). Red wine has been shown to increase HDL (good cholesterol) which in turn, reduces LDL (bad cholesterol), again, only if used in moderation as previously described. In excess (more than 10 ounces per day for men, and more than five ounces for women), has been shown to be detrimental to one's health from the above described reasons.

"**Saturated fats:** Saturated fats, or bad fats, are directly linked to cardiovascular disease (heart attacks and strokes), and some cancers (possibly breast, definitively prostate and small intestinal cancers). Foods that are 'deep fried,' or foods with butter, coconut oil, cream, cheese, chocolate, and ground beef tend to be high in saturated fats) The effects of saturated fats are in direct contrast to the effects of unsaturated non-trans fats (found in things such as olive oil, vegetable oil, avocado's, soy, and nuts). Unsaturated non-trans fats are beneficial at increasing HDL (good cholesterol) and reducing LDL (bad cholesterol), but must still be taken in sparingly because of their high caloric content. To simplify things, look for the label 'hydrogenated or partially hydrogenated' and avoid these foods, because they tend to have high saturated (bad) fat contents. Children (under age two) *should not be on low fat diets, because they need both saturated/ unsaturated fats for brain development.*

*"**Salt:** Sodium intake should not exceed about one and a half teaspoons a day! (2300mg). Our bodies need salt, but the average diet (even vegan or vegetarian diets) will supply the necessary amount of salt. Even natural foods have some natural quantities of sodium, so one teaspoon adds up fast. Any foods that are 'preserved,' are guaranteed to be high in salt, and fast food generally is high in salt as well. Excess salt intake has been directly linked to hypertension, cardiovascular disease (heart attacks and strokes), kidney disease (or kidney failure), water retention (edema)."*

All these food products are produced in mass quantities and are advertised directly to our youth as well as communities in their entirety. This means the very old to those just old enough to walk and understand are consuming these foods. If we were aware of the harmful effects of such consumables, what rationale would be plausible for our continual feeding of ourselves and our youth with such rations?

As we saturate ourselves with soda pop, potato chips, various saturated fats, and acids, which does much harm to our bodies and those of our youth, we allow ourselves to become part and parcel to multibillion dollar industries. These industries that are only too happy to supply us with what our bodies don't need, but what they overwhelmingly convince our minds that we require to satisfy our insatiable appetites.

Recently the Center for Science in the Public Interest published an article online titled, *Soft Drinks Undermining Americans' Health: Teens Consuming Twice as Much 'Liquid Candy' as Milk.* According to this report, *"Teenage boys and girls drink twice as much soda pop as milk, whereas 20 years ago they drank nearly twice as much milk as soda."*

According to this report, teens drink great quantities of soda, which is referred to as "Liquid Candy." The Center for Science in the Public Interest (CSPI) reported that government data revealed that the average 12- to 19-year-old male consumes more than two cans of soda per day, while the average female in the same age group consumes 1¾ cans a day.

To make their point, *"At a press conference in Washington, D.C., the nonprofit CSPI displayed the 868 cans of soda pop that the average 12- to 19-year male soda drinker drinks annually."*

"CSPI's new analyses of 13- to 18-year-olds found that five percent of male soft-drink drinkers down about five or more cans a day and five percent of female drinkers consume more than three cans a day. That's 80 percent more than 20 years ago.

"Overall, Americans are consuming twice as much soda pop as they did 25 years ago. And they're spending $54 billion a year on it. That's twice what Americans spend on books."

In this report Dr. Bess Dawson-Hughes stated that she was really concerned about teenage girls because they tend to not consume enough calcium. Replacing milk with soda worsens this problem. This lack of calcium will make them vulnerable to suffering broken bones and osteoporosis later in life. Others have expressed concern that research shows soda consumption may increase the risk of developing kidney stones in men, and may also increase the risk of developing heart disease in both male and female adults. It was further noted that soft drinks such as Surge, a product of the Coca-Cola Company, may provide a form of legal stimulant for many teenagers. Even diet soft drinks may pose a health hazard to both teens and adults. For example, artificial sweeteners such as acesulfame-K and saccharin are viewed as possible cancer-causing agents.

For more information visit the Center for Science in the Public Interest via this link: https://cspinet.org/eating-healthy.

Many foods and other consumables weaken us; the pharmaceutical industry then medicates, but does little to cure us; the medical profession practices on us, and then turns us over to the morticians to dispose of us. It appears as if we are industry livestock. In a manner, we are!

We produce and provide the foods our youth consume. We go to stores and purchase food rations and bring them into our homes to feed our youth. As adults, we target our marketing and advertising toward our youth. If what we targeted toward them was good for them and would bring better heath, promote or increase vigor and vitality, our efforts would thus be noble and praiseworthy. However, that is not always the case. Often, the opposite is true.

Also, the way we prepare meals is usually passed from generation to generation. Cooking high saturated fat or salty meals can become so familiar in the home that no one realizes the dangers until someone becomes ill. My eating habits are picked up by my sons and daughters as I received them from my parents. When I practice healthy habits, my offspring reproduce the same practices and teach them to their young as well. However, if my consumption traditions are shaped by Industrialists who concern themselves only with their bottom line, what good is it for me and my family? If mass production and reducing costs along with advertising to gain the highest profit margin shape my eating habits, what have my offspring acquired? If we buy into such an arrangement, who wins and who loses? If we follow the industrialist model, has my family's future fitness model gained vitality, or is it headed in a more destructive direction?

We work hard to pay our bills and ensure that our youth have what they need. Yet we fill ourselves with steady diets of fast foods that are weakening and killing us and them.

Most commonly, adults are the producers of the foods that we ourselves eat as well as feed to our youth. In the pursuit of higher profit margins, manufactures cut production quality in just about every industry, including food production. We feed our youth junk by the millions of tons per year and wonder why they are obese. We wonder why we have the "dumbing down" affect commonly noted by researchers in test scores nationwide. When we shortcut the sustenance necessary for our bodies to function at optimal proficiency, we do a great disservice to ourselves and future generations. Many of the same individuals who give their kids pop and potato chips only use high octane gas in their cars. Go figure! By providing less than healthy foods we cut short the very thing that we should hold most precious, our own lives and the lives of our youth and their offspring. Foods are intended to energize, sustain, and increase vitality and longevity, not break it down.

Sidebar: *We impart to our younger generation messages that even confuse me. How can we imagine that they will take hold of a firm understanding of truth when we give coded messages but have not been successful in providing the decoder?*

Fair Play

When a young person gets into trouble and the other person who participated with them in their dirty work doesn't get caught, you hear them say, *"That's not fair!"* Fair play seems to be something that young people believe in and desire. While everything in life is not fair, some things are particularly glaring and stand out as symbols of injustice.

Court systems which preclude true justice are an affront to the dignity of a society, and these injustices are not concealed from young people's recognition. What do you believe young people perceive as it relates to buying and selling justice or parceling it out based on anything other than the facts of the case?

Sidebar: *Flowing water will seek out the path of least resistance. Whatever path is laid, the water will course through and pool at the lowest level. Likewise, we lay the course and our youth flow accordingly. Do we cut the low path or will we take the high road?*

So many things in life that seem to be second nature or naturally occurring conditions are oftentimes not as worthwhile as that which requires toil, thought, experimentation and exploration. Exploration of our minds and inner qualities only come forward as a result of tapping into that part of us that only God can enumerate. Such quantification comes about by purging off the dross through fire and the testing of our metal. As a society of individuals, communities, nations and unquestionably the entire world, we must begin to look earnestly into ourselves and reach for that which can only be of assistance collectively to us all. By all, I mean everyone who has ever lived and those living now, followed by those who will live after us. We have traveled down the road of *"me, myself, and I"* much too far. The days of *"I got mine and I don't care about you,"* must be over and done away with.

We've missed too many opportunities to teach our children important values about preservation of a sacred culture, a valiant and charitable people, nobility, integrity, truth and righteousness. We must endeavor to be that which we were created to be, a community dedicated to seeking truth and the common good. There have always been pockets of good surrounded by domineering wickedness worldwide. Those who uphold right living beliefs must speak aloud those precepts with one mighty voice and teach true goodness diligently to our youth who will carry them on into future generations. We must see them move in a moral and ethical path to make for a world without the degree of moral contamination and decay such as we see today. When we scrutinize the current events portrayed in our daily news we clearly can see a necessity for change and refocus. We are on an unsustainable heading which must be altered for the good of those who follow behind us.

We need only look back to past failings as well as successes to see where humanity is heading. Remember that past practice is a great indicator of future tendencies. Even though it is not locked or static, it is a powerful indicator which cannot be dismissed. We still have freedom of choice! No matter where we are at present we can always select an alternative route.

What have we done which is lasting, good and virtuous? What can we lay claim to that truly makes the world today and future generations superior to past generations? Of course, we have greater technological advancements, more powerful weaponry, faster food preparation, better pharmaceuticals, homes and cars. Our space exploration programs have provided humanity with a greater understanding of the world and the so-called universe in which we live. We have geology, biology, veterinary science and many other disciplines by which we gain knowledge of ourselves and the world around us.

How do we utilize the information we've gained to make us wiser or provide ourselves with more integrity? As individuals, we need to build our inner qualities such as love, peace of mind, the ability to forgive. Are we moving towards God or away from God? Are we more friendly or less friendly than our fore-parents were in the society in which they lived? What behavior must we as a generation admit to that was wicked, heinous, or depraved? And are we at a point that we can begin to repent and move in a direction towards wholeness collectively and teach such principals diligently to our youth? Today's news headlines will bring lucidity and a sense of where we are and where we are heading. Where to go from here should be the all-consuming question, ready upon all our hearts once we have apprehended an understanding of our present position.

Much good has been done in the world by individuals who possess understanding and who operate in a higher paradigm than most. There is much good in the world today which to some extent goes unnoticed as it gets buried under the enormity of negative reports and scandals. If the daily news reporters would only share some of that good news more often, perhaps our world would be a nicer place to live!

Chapter Eleven

You're Up To Bat

Imagine this scene: bottom of the ninth and you're on deck and the pitcher is throwing some real heat. Each toss causes the catcher to take off his catcher's mitt to check to see if his hand is OK. Yup, his hand is red and swollen as he suspected.

You're on deck as you watch the batter get caught looking as his final strike screams over the plate, and the ump yells *"Strike three, you're out!"* Nervously you walk up to the batter's box with two outs and three on base. You think about how many of your teammates are getting struck out. You think about how the hits that your teammates have gotten were merely pop flies that were easily caught by the outfielder. Or they are grounders that the shortstop scoops up and throws swiftly to the first baseman and the ump yells emphatically, *"Out!"*

All your team's hits came in the first and second inning, but lately the opposing team is pitching a shutout and has closed the gap; their pitcher is on a streak. The game could go either way as the score is very close. All the spectators are looking at you. Half of them are yelling *"Boooo, throw the bum out,"* and the other half are hoping that you will hit it out of the park and bring in those runners already on base.

Each generation (or inning) before that of today's youth made some runs. In fact, they did very well, but in the middle to late innings many errors were made in the field. So many dropped balls! So many times the third baseman was looking the other way as the ball came screaming past him. So many times, the second baseman refused to throw the ball to the first baseman because he didn't want to see the first baseman get the accolades of tagging the runner out. After all, I stopped the ball so the camera should be on me, he thinks to himself. There's too much disharmony and infighting on the field and in the locker room, with contract disputes and jealousy about other teammate's money. There are too many players without any commitment to the team or dedication to having a winning season. The only thing that matters is that they look good in uniform. These and so many other distractions became the norm while the season was still in progress.

However, the bases are loaded and a grand slam would win the game here in the bottom of the ninth — and finally you're up to bat! Even though you have come up from the minor league, all eyes are on you. Circumstance and timing have thrust you into the limelight. Without you no victory will be won.

Now you're up and the pitcher looks intently at you as if he knows he is going to strike you out, just as he has so many others before you. He clearly plans to win this all-important game for his team. If you hit anything less than a homerun our team losses this make or break game. As you raise the bat into position above your head with your knees slightly bent, you have your eyes fixed intently into the pitcher's eyes. The pitcher is fixed ever so desirously on you as well. He is nearly foaming at the mouth with yearnings to sift you, demolish you, to destroy and obliterate you.

He knows that winning against you is his big chance to close the game. You are now ready to take your first swing at the fire the pitcher is throwing; the game rests in your hands. The pitcher studies you long and hard, then he contorts his powerful looking body as he winds up to throw the first pitch. It is a 195 mile per hour fast ball curve sink slider pitch. It's a blur as it goes straight over the plate. You swing but miss miserably. *"Strike one,"* the umpire shouts! Unseen hellish spectators fiendishly howl with delight, as you appear to be at the pitcher's mercy. You now understand that you will have to bring all the knowhow that you have at your disposal to get a hit with what this pitcher is throwing.

Now, it seems like the entire dugout gathers on the mound to confer with the pitcher because they understand the significance of this next pitch. They want to get you behind early so that all the advantage is on their side. When the group on the mound disperses, the terrible tosser looks hard at you. His eyes ablaze as his chest rises and falls with each heavy breath he takes. He has his planned throw firmly fixed in his mind. After his conference with his teammates at the mound, those teammates of his who have scouted you from your youth and studied all your tendencies, they know the perfect pitch to throw just for you that would certainly entice you to swing.

He then adjusts his crotch and spits out a foul looking substance before he winds up for the next throw. Once again, he contorts his impressive hulking mass as he winds up to heave another terrifying pitch, and this time it's a 205 mph reverse curve fast ball turn around pitch.

You can barely see the ball, but you blindly swing. Thwack! You hit it flush, you don't know how but you did. Your bat shatters into splinters as the ball sails past third. Back, back, back goes the outfielder as he tries to grab it to place the game on ice. You drop what's left of your bat and commence running towards first base as fast as you can. Down the first base line you dart as you watch the outfielders attempt to catch the ball. What a hit! What a giant smack you placed on that ball! It's a wonder that the cover is still on it! As the ball comes down it's very close to the foul line, but the outfielder is determined. He knows that if he catches your pop fly; foul or not, you are out and they win. You reach first base and strain your neck to see if your ball will be caught. The outfielder stretches for it with all that he's got, but at the last second, he trips and falls just as the ball drops outside the third baseline. Foul!

Now it's two strikes and no balls. Slowly you walk back to the batter's box. You doubt that you can ever hit anything this pitcher is throwing again. You felt so lucky to hit it the last time, and now you must go back and try again. *"Damn, damn, damn,"* you think to yourself. In your mind you are also thinking, *"I want to go home. I don't want to do this. The pressure is too great."* However, you resolve that you must stand in there and give it your all. So back into the batter's box you go. You stand there intimidated, not wanting to look at the pitcher's fiery stare, not wanting him to recognize your disquieted heart.

Nervously holding the bat down, you step out of the batter's box and take off your cap, wiping the perspiration from your brow. Understanding the importance of what is to come you contemplate every possible outcome of your actions. The tension has mounted to the point that uncertainty is at its apex, you don't know what the outcome will be. But you step back into the box to await the next pitch. Anxiety resulting from the pressure of everyone's expectation has you hoping, yet doubting. You're relying on your strengths; you're trusting in the fact that you can do what is necessary to win the day. Yet uncertainty abounds. Mentally you struggle to hold your focus.

Seventh-Inning Stretch Has Begun!

Youth and their offspring will see us through to our ultimate destination as a race of human beings. It is inevitable that, all that human beings were created to be will someday surface. We have traveled the road we are presently trudging for millennia with the climax now firmly fixed in our sites. Those of us within a relatively mature age grouping may or may not physically see the Christ's return, or the culmination of human existence on Earth. We can, however, discern what will be a most probable outcome if we stay on our present path. Results of the course we have set out on are predictable; the Manual has also foretold of outcomes.

Unless we plot a new course or otherwise redirect ourselves, we will undoubtedly succeed to our expected destination of ruin. Apart from Christ as our Commander-in-Chief, we flounder as a ship without rudder or sail. Fortunately, the prophecy foretells of His triumphant reentrance just in the nick of time. We look forward to that with the upmost optimism. Read what has been written about the last days in 2 Timothy 3:1-9 of the Manual:

"But mark this: There will be terrible times in the last days. People will be lovers of themselves, lovers of money, boastful, proud, abusive, disobedient to their parents, ungrateful, unholy, without love, unforgiving, slanderous, without self-control, brutal, not lovers of the good, treacherous, rash, and conceited, lovers of pleasure rather than lovers of God, having a form of godliness but denying its power. Have nothing to do with them."

My friend, this is a perfect description of present times; we have but to look around us to see it. Young men and young women, do not be afraid of who you truly are. More importantly, do not be deceived into becoming that which you are not. You have a great destiny and there is a grand purpose which can and will be performed only through you. Mankind is on assignment here on Earth, now just as it has been from the beginning. In Genesis 1:22, when referring to mankind it says that God blessed them and said to them:

"Be fruitful and increase in number; fill the earth and subdue it. Rule over the fish of the sea and the birds of the air and over every living creature that moves on the ground." Moreover, we find in the Book of Matthew 28:16-20, it says, *"Then the eleven disciples went to Galilee, to the mountain where Jesus had told*

them to go. When they saw Him, they worshiped Him; but some doubted. Then Jesus came to them and said, 'All authority in heaven and on earth has been given to me. Therefore, go and make disciples of all nations, baptizing them in the name of the Father and of the Son and of the Holy Spirit, and teaching them to obey everything I have commanded you. And surely, I am with you always, to the very end of the age.'"

Reproducing what God has produced, and bringing continued order into being with the authority given us, seems to be one of our chief duties. You, young man and young lady, will bring all of God's human family into fellowship with the light. For as it says in 1 Thessalonians 4:13-18 of the Manual:

"Brothers, we do not want you to be ignorant about those who fall asleep, or to grieve like the rest of men, who have no hope. We believe that Jesus died and rose again and so we believe that God will bring with Jesus those who have fallen asleep in him. According to the Lord's own word, we tell you that we who are still alive, who are left till the coming of the Lord, will certainly not precede those who have fallen asleep. For the Lord Himself will come down from heaven, with a loud command, with the voice of the archangel and with the trumpet call of God, and the dead in Christ will rise first. After that, we who are still alive and are left will be caught up together with them in the clouds to meet the Lord in the air. And so we will be with the Lord forever. Therefore encourage each other with these words."

To see the things that you will see and participate in the restoration of all things as you one day will, is a highly prized future for which providence has selected you. Do not shrink from it, retreat or doubt! Do not fear or hesitate! Not for a moment! Rather embrace the true call which is yours to fulfill, and find your Father the glorious God of righteousness who awaits our arrival which, apart from you, will not be complete.

Therefore, understand the patriarchs and matriarchs of the faith, such as Abraham, Isaac and Jacob, David, Mary and Joseph, Daniel and Joshua, Ester, Moses, Elizabeth, Noah and Jonah as well. Embrace the progenitors of our family trees, our great-great-grandmothers and great-great-grandfathers, those who gave way under the heavy hand of slavery while trusting the Lord that one day God would deliver them. Study the Founding Fathers of this great nation, sisters and brothers, those who passed through this life in hardship having faith in God; slain profits and fallen pastors who toiled tirelessly for the cause of Christ, having been gathered to their fathers and are now resting. Do not forget your cohorts who look to you for inspiration and encouragement, those who read your life as an open book, your children and your yet unborn who are still in your eggs or seeds, are all jointly in reliance upon you. You can do all through your strength who is Christ. Youth is not wasted on the young but your exuberance and zest for life are merely indications that the task set before you require energy, creativity, strength and resilience. You are so ready to assume positions of leadership, victoriously having overcome the world, the flesh, and our common enemy.

Sidebar: *"So many people walk around with a meaningless life. They seem half-asleep, even when they're busy doing things they think are important. This is because they're chasing the wrong things. The way you get meaning into your life is to devote yourself to loving others, devote yourself to your community around you, and devote yourself to creating something that gives you purpose and meaning."* — Morrie Schwartz

The world is as a steady current, vehemently beating against our inner being, attempting to force us into submission and compliance to an unholy kingdom whose ruler is the Evil One. As it says in Revelation 12:7-12 of the Manual: *"And there was war in heaven, Michael and his angels fought against the dragon, and the dragon and his angels fought back but he was not strong enough, and they lost their place in heaven. The great dragon was hurled down — that ancient serpent called the devil, or Satan, who leads the whole world astray. He was hurled to the earth, and his angels with him.*

"Then I heard a loud voice in heaven say: "Now have come the salvation and the power and the kingdom of our God, and the authority of his Christ. For the accuser of our brothers, who accuses them before our God day and night, has been hurled down. They overcame him by the blood of the Lamb and by the word of their testimony; they did not love their lives so much as to shrink from death. Therefore, rejoice you heavens and you who dwell in them! But woe to the earth and the sea, because the devil has gone down to you! He is filled with fury, because he knows that his time is short."

Have you taken notice of what's happening in our world today? The conversation of our friends, co-workers, or our family will tell you just how dire we find our current situation. The news stories are magnified by our telling and retelling of the gruesome headlines to each other. The appalling acts reported in the headlines are performed by individuals who are directed by unseen forces of darkness. They have been influenced to do whatever it is that they did by the demonic forces that are unseen, but quite impactful in our world. Of course, you already know that:

"Our struggle is not against flesh and blood, but against the rulers, against the authorities, against the powers of this dark world and against the spiritual forces of evil in the heavenly realms. Therefore, put on the full armor of God, so that when the day of evil comes, you may be able to stand your ground, and after you have done everything, to stand." — Ephesians 6:12-13 of the Instruction Manual.

The flesh causes us to lust after the things that bring only self-satisfaction, most often at the expense of doing the things that we know are spiritually bolstering. Inside we know the difference between right and wrong, good or bad. Our fleshly bodies compel us to bring to it worldly fulfillment and are constantly struggling against our spiritual bodies — which is the part of us connected to God. What does it say about this in the Instruction Manual? Let us see. In the Book of Romans 8:4-14 it states that:

"The righteousness of the law might be fulfilled in us, who walk not after the flesh, but after the Spirit. For they that are after the flesh do mind the things of the flesh; but they that are after the Spirit the things of the Spirit. For to be carnally minded is death; but to be spiritually minded is life and peace. Because the carnal mind is enmity against God: for it is not subject to the law of God, neither indeed can be. So then they that are in the flesh cannot please God. But you are not in the flesh, but in the Spirit, if so be that the Spirit of God dwell in you. Now if any man has not the Spirit of Christ, he is none of his. And if Christ be in you, the body is dead because of sin; but the Spirit is life because of righteousness. But if the Spirit of Him that raised up Jesus from the dead dwell in you, He that raised up Christ from the dead shall also quicken your mortal bodies by His Spirit that dwells in you. Therefore, brethren, we are debtors, not to the flesh, to live after the flesh. For if ye live after the flesh, ye shall die: but if ye through the Spirit do mortify the deeds of the body, ye shall live. For as many as are led by the Spirit of God, they are the sons of God."

The Manual further states in Romans 7:21-25:

"So I find this law at work: When I want to do good, evil is right there with me. For in my inner being I delight in God's law; but I see another law at work in the members of my body, waging war against the law of my mind and making me a

prisoner of the law of sin at work within my members. What a wretched man I am! Who will rescue me from this body of death? Thanks be to God — through Jesus Christ our Lord!"

Consequently, we can understand that there is indeed a struggle going on within us. In a sense, arresting us and leading us away from the liberty and freedom apportioned each of us, and confining us to lodgings in places of moral incarceration. Our Creator has a superior purpose for you, plans to prosper you and to bring you to an expected end. He has sent our freedom from these bonds of detention in the person of the CHRIST, the one anointed of God. Our common enemy has attempted to thwart the Master's plans from the outset by deceiving us into accepting less and believing that we are less than what we have been created to be.

Now open your eyes and you will see the light of God's presence; do not fear or hesitate. Stand in the light of God's truth and be who you are — mighty sons and daughters of the MOST HIGH GOD! Fueled by the power of the Holy Spirit, no weapon formed against you shall prosper. If God be for you, who can stand against you?

What has been taking place for generations has been intended to be a set up for your failure as you reach for the golden ring of end time victory. Our failures and mistakes, the misfortunes of our parents and their parents before them, all have set you up to strike out when it really counts. Conversely, the greatest victory of all time can also be won in times of adversity — times when it will take a miracle to win! These are the times that God steps into circumstances. The Lord of glory has put into place a way to escape this strategic plot by our enemy, which is the planned downfall of us all. Do not allow yourselves to fall for that same old scheme that the devil has been running on humans for eons. The old bait and switch; it looks good until you grab it, only to find you have placed your hand in a snare and now you are bound by the reality behind the false image you so desired to be true.

Picture if you will a marathon where runners give themselves tirelessly as they run for miles over long stretches of difficult terrain, day after arduous day. As the race progresses an unscrupulous competitor sets traps near the finish line because he knows that he cannot win by fair or conventional methods. As you feel the home stretch getting nearer you also feel the weariness of having run so long and your will and energy are weakening. This cheater has watched the films of you and has studied your every tendency. He knows your weak points and understands the optimum timing necessary to trip you. He also knows the areas of your strength and has attempted with all due diligence to keep you disconnected from that strength.

He has provided distractions and diversions of entertainment along the way, all the more as the finish line comes nearer into view. Within the last 40 years we have seen a sharp spike in such distractions.

The boom of video game technology, new and innovative television, DVD, Blu-ray equipment, along with music and the unending stream of movies and music make it clear that we are being entertained out of our minds. We now find MP3 players and IPod, cell phone technology, and laptop and home PC systems in almost every home. We see gigantic monitors for viewing events, ads, and other entertainment as we walk down the street in some large cities. Porn shops lining the streets, sports frenzy and non-stop TV and Internet streaming into every home 24/7 are all part of today's reality.

This enemy has bought off the officials and laid booby traps in your lane. As you may know, a booby trap is a trap designed to kill or severely injure a human. As the word "trap" implies, they often have some form of bait designed to lure the victim towards it. He is determined to defeat you. The runner in this scenario is humanity and the unscrupulous competitor is the enemy of mankind, the Evil One!

For ages, he has awaited the time when you were completely distracted and your focus was at an all-time low, a time when he had sufficiently convinced you that there was no enemy because he stayed in the shadows along the path setting the stage for the finish line. He has trusted that by now you will question if there is a Heavenly Father or a Holy Spirit aiding you along the journey because he has consistently registered subliminal messages that you are all alone.

Sidebar: Nobody in here but us chickens! There is no such thing as a devil, that's just made up stuff for horror movies. As far as the world goes that's just how it is in these days and times. Get with it old timer, we don't believe in that antiquated stuff no more. It's time for people to put away those superstitions and ancient myths about the gods, and trying to put restrictions on others, right? Everybody should be free to choose the way they want to live for themselves. According to whom? The Almighty Father always instructed us, so who do you suppose is now saying "Do your own thing?"

Now the perfect snare has been laid; it's ready to catapult you to the ground. If you go down your enemy would pounce on you, never to allow you to arise again for fear of the power you truly do possess. Open your mind and your understanding and allow the unscrupulous dragon to be revealed for what he has always been, what he is now and will continue to be in the future.

Now with his smokescreen unmasked, he knows that you see him for the deceiver he has always been, and that you would not allow yourself to be lulled into complacency for another hundred thousand eons. Hence, you must realize that this is his moment and seize it he must! He has invested everything into your deception for your destruction. Everything will come to a point in time together. The Lord will bring his armies according to Revelation 16:12-21 of the Manual:

"The sixth angel poured out his bowl on the great river Euphrates, and its water was dried up to prepare the way for the kings from the East. Then I saw three evil spirits that looked like frogs; they came out of the mouth of the dragon, out of the mouth of the beast and out of the mouth of the false prophet. They are spirits of demons performing miraculous signs, and they go out to the kings of the whole world, to gather them for the battle on the great day of God Almighty. 'Behold, I come like a thief! Blessed is he who stays awake and keeps his clothes with him, so that he may not go naked and be shamefully exposed.' Then they gathered the kings together to the place that in Hebrew is called Armageddon. The seventh angel poured out his bowl into the air, and out of the temple came a loud voice from the throne, saying, 'It is done!' Then there came flashes of lightning, rumblings, peals of thunder and a severe earthquake. No earthquake like it has ever occurred since man has been on earth, so tremendous was the quake. The great city split into three parts, and the cities of the nations collapsed. God remembered Babylon the Great and gave her the cup filled with the wine of the fury of His wrath. Every island fled away and the mountains could not be found. From the sky huge hailstones of about a hundred pounds each fell upon men. And they cursed God on account of the plague of hail, because the plague was so terrible."

Our common enemy, the Evil One, also has a purpose and a plan for your life. His schemes are fiendishly plotted to interrupt the flow of God's perfect love towards and through you. He plans to corrupt you with his destructive vices, and ultimately have the Lord send you with him and his demonic legion to the bottomless pit when Christ ultimately vanquishes him once and for all time. In the Book of Job 1:7 we see the Evil One conversing with God about his being on the Earth. *"And the Lord said to Satan, 'Where have you come from? Satan answered the Lord, from roaming through the earth and going back and forth in it.'"* Again, according to the Instruction Manual (1 Peter 5:8-9) we are admonished to be self-controlled and alert: *"Your enemy the devil prowls around like a roaring lion looking for someone to devour. Resist him, standing firm in the faith, because you know that your brothers throughout the world are undergoing the same kind of sufferings."*

We see in the Book of Mathew 4:1-11 of the Manual, *"Then Jesus was led by the Spirit into the desert to be tempted by the devil. After fasting forty days and forty nights, He was hungry. The tempter came to Him and said, 'If you are the Son of God, tell these stones to become bread.'*

"Jesus answered, 'It is written: Man does not live on bread alone, but on every word that comes from the mouth of God.' Then the devil took Him to the holy city and had Him stand on the highest point of the temple. 'If you are the Son of God,' he said, 'throw yourself down. For it is written: He will command his angels concerning you' and, 'they will lift you up in their hands, so that you will not strike your foot against a stone.' Jesus answered him, 'it is also written: Do not put the Lord your God to the test.' Again, the devil took Him to a very high mountain and showed Him all the kingdoms of the world and their splendor. 'All this I will give you,' he said, 'if you will bow down and worship me.' Jesus said to him, 'Away from me, Satan! For it is written: Worship the Lord your God, and serve Him only.' Then the devil left him, and angels came and attended Him."

How can we hoodwink ourselves into believing that we are not being impacted by the enemy when we see that even Jesus Himself was taken by Satan to a place and was tempted? Mighty Michael and his valiant warrior companion angels fought against the dragon and his angels. They fought back, but they were not strong enough, and they lost their place in heaven. Michael is very courageous and mighty and he had to fight the devil, and by all indications he had to fight most fiercely.

From this we must conclude that Satan is a formidable foe, one to be reckoned with and not dismissed as a myth or a non-existing creation of our forefather's fears. We have received instructions in the Book of Ephesians, 6-11:

"Be strong in the Lord and in His mighty power. Put on the full armor of God so that you can take your stand against the devil's schemes."

Time is of the essence, it is short and most priceless, so don't waste a moment of it. Move forward expeditiously and purpose-fully, knowing that the enemy to your life has set perfect snares in your path. Like so many generations before you, the enemy intends that you will also be trapped and rendered ineffective. God has prepared the more excellent way of escape from the snares of the enemy through Yahushua, the Christ. However, be sure that the generational difficulties that have transferred from countless parents to offspring down through the years will end once and for all with you. You are a chosen generation, a royal priesthood. Be strong and very courageous; with God you can do all things. Trust in the Lord with all your heart and lean not on your own understandings. In all your ways acknowledge Him, and He will make your paths straight. Do not be wise in your own eyes; fear the Lord and shun evil. This will bring health to your body and nourishment to your bones. Honor the Lord with your wealth, with the first fruits of all your increase; then your barns will be filled to overflowing, and your vats will overflow. So says the Manual of earthly living.

Seventh-Inning Stretch Has Ended!

Let's get back to the game as it is hotly contested and everything is on the line. As you come up to the plate to take your next swing, do not fear, for fear is one of our enemy's choicest weapons. Look him confidently in the eye knowing that heaven and Earth will pass away before God's word does — and God's word has declared you the victor. We are not confident in our own might but the strength of the Lord. The same one who created all the heavens above and the Earth below, the stars, sun, and the moon, is the one who empowers you. God created you and me in His image and His likeness and called for us to have authority on this Earth, even as it is in heaven. When that ball comes across the plate with all vigor and concentration, take a level swing trusting in God's might that now courses in you through His Holy Spirit.

Now with the climax of this struggle playing out before all the heavens and the Earth, suddenly the crowd is hushed and everyone is looking upward. Triumphantly a glorious rider steps in as the replacement batter. With him he brings a whole new cheering section brilliantly attired. As the stands are already filled, this new cheering section now fills the skies. They begin singing a victory song as if the game is over and they have already won. The new batter rode down from above, this majestic pinch hitter looks intently into your eyes with a gaze that pierced your soul, leaving you extraordinarily different somehow. He placed his hand on your shoulder, leaned in toward you in somewhat of an embrace. He then whispered in your ear, *"Well done good soldier, hit the showers, I got this."*

You walk off the field with the greatest feeling of relief and gladness, knowing that you are now out of the hot seat and he has taken your place. You couldn't help looking back at him as you walk off the field. You whisper *"Thank you"* to yourself over and over as you look back at him. As you enter the dugout you see how your teammates are looking at you and realize you had not been whispering at all but shouting your gratitude to the glorious rider. You didn't care that the others looked at you this way. You were simply refreshed and overwhelmed with gladness. He had lifted the weight of the moment from your shoulders. They didn't understand like you did what he had done for you.

He then takes the bat and knocks the dirt from his shoes. Suddenly the other team is very nervous and they begin to scurry around with pensive uncertain movements. The team's captain, who had pitched so solidly, is now removed from the mound by the team skipper, the commander from of old, the prince of this world. From out of the shadows he comes. Finally, he reveals himself to battle this majestic pinch hitter. At this point no chances will be taken. Only the all-stars are on the outfield now. A real showdown is taking place. What a universal spectacle!

The skipper takes the ball himself. It has been said that he knows every pitch in the book as well as every pitch that is not in the book. With focused intent, the batter and the pitcher look at each other as with a familiar recognition. Yes, they know each other. The batter also knows every pitch in or out of the book; moreover, he knows how to hit each one. This toss is going to be for the game and all the marbles. At first there was a hush throughout the stadium, but now the stands and the skies are abuzz with clamor. With shouting and very noisome tension this moment is beyond anything history can recall. With even more brashness and obdurate pride and stubbornness, this new pitcher takes the mound. His appearance is splendid indeed. He looks impeccable as he adjusts himself and leads into his windup.

The batter looks confidently superior to anything we have ever viewed as he stands in the box. His eyes strangely fixed upward as if he is in no way concerned. It almost looks as if he is talking to someone, and when he opens his mouth, razor sharp looking swords dart out. His eyes appear as the sun, blazing as fire. And instead of a ball cap he has a great number of crowns on his head. Also, he isn't wearing a tradition ball uniform, but some sort of robe or something. And the name on his uniform says **Faithful and True.**

This dazzling vision of splendor and all those who came with him are similarly dressed in these brilliantly white outfits. But his robe seems to have been dipped in what appears to be blood. There is something unbelievable in this moment, yet it is happening. This is no ordinary batter, no indeed! Someone said that when he arrived he rode in on a white steed. Obviously, something about that is ringing true because everybody saw it and those who came with him are still mounted as if ready to battle. They are holding formation up near the clouds in anticipation of the next pitch. What an awesome sight! Also on his robe and on his thigh, he has a name written, it says *"King of Kings and Lord of Lords."* No, this batter is not ordinary at all! He is absolutely extraordinary indeed!

The pitcher, now concluding his astounding windup, throws a never before seen or heard of 360 sink slide elevator curve fast ball at a whopping 365 mph. He put his all into the pitch, fully attempting to get it over the plate and past the batter. He laid it all on the line. The ball appeared to disappear in the millisecond it took for the ball to cross the plate. This was the pitch that was saved especially for this occasion.

But, the blazing watchful eyes of the great batter, **Faithful and True,** never lost sight of it. He lined it up with his bat at the same time that the pitcher released the ball. He swung with passion and power. The sound of the bat meeting the ball was heard around the world and throughout the universe as the ball was hit flush. Up, up, up it went, out of the park, over the stands, beyond the clouds and over the rainbow. The ball flew with such force it created some sort of vortex vacuum that extracted all the other team's players and their fans as it screamed out of the park. Where the ball and all those individuals went, God only knows! It has been reported that there was a pit without bottom far beyond the playing field that hungrily received them. No one can catch the ball ***Faithful and True*** hit. It was indeed the most amazing thing ever.

Now, all in attendance at the great spectacle have been fortified by the supreme highest. I see the runners who were on base turning the bases and coming home. Each one arriving to a glorious welcome as they touched home plate. Grandma and grandpa, mom and dad, they are all coming down the third base line and tagging the home plate. Martin Luther King, Jr. and John Fitzgerald Kennedy appear at home plate and tag the bag. Gandhi, Joseph, Mary and Martha, Queen Ester and Mordechai, all follow. Daniel, Sampson, and Noah, all round the bases and tag the bag.

Such a great number of individuals joyfully exclaiming *"He has done it, He has done it!"* Crowds gathered around, jubilation erupts with praise and singing, dancing and shouting. The clouds are abuzz with clamor and activity as the host of heaven rejoices. This long awaited and expected outcome has finally squashed this insurrection. ***Faithfull and True***, the hero of the game, was raised upon the shoulders of all his teammates and fans. All that were in the stands shouted and heaped praise onto him shouting, *"How glorious, how wonderful, there is none greater, he is the victor."* They shouted *"We will follow him wherever he leads us! Hosanna, Hosanna, Hosanna!"*

It has finally been concluded, and not without your participation, young brother and little sister! Thank you for bringing us home! Thank you for standing in the batter's box when it mattered most. You are to be applauded for your refusal to break under the pressure of bending. The integrity of your faith has provided the wherewithal for you to stand. Bending is understandable given the circumstances, but you did not break!

Finally, my brothers and sisters, as you play in the final inning of this great struggle, you see the grand slam homer sail out of the park. You are completely fastened together with *Faithful and True*, turning around third base together. You can see home coming into view. The crowd is urging you on toward home plate, hands clapping, hands raised, overwhelming joy, and true happiness with unspeakable delight and fulfillment.

For in you resides the power of Christ's own mighty right arm, and not by your own might or by your power, but by His spirit you will make it home and you will help bring us all in as well.

Never be found doubting that He will see you through to this triumphant homecoming. He has readied you for this moment since time began. You are well equipped for the task and you will succeed, I assure you!

What you must understand is there is a way that the world has not embraced; against all resistance you must prevail to embrace this way and make it your daily practice. Love the Lord with all your heart, soul and mind, and be careful not to be enticed into the adoption of falsehood so that the flood of the Lord's blessing will not terminate in your life. Your blessings will be passed on to the generations following you as the Lord reigns.

The way of the world is a noose, readied to hang those who place their necks within it. Consider generations that have passed before you, and see where an uncle or aunt, grandparent, friend, or acquaintance followed after the world's vice, love of money, or the pleasure principal. Think of what the earthly end of that person was or who got burned because of their pursuits.

Contemplate for a moment if you will your own life. Will you finish well? Who will be blessed or burned because of you being in their lives? How will the world benefit from you being placed on this Earth? Really stop now, ponder and answer these questions to yourself alone. You can avail yourselves of every opportunity to give or receive good things and be triumphantly successful. Do so! You are God's creation so love yourself, give of yourself to others. Your cohorts are God's creations also. Receive them in the spirit of gratitude, love, and appreciation. Join in the spirit of truth. Love God with all your heart, mind, and soul, and love your neighbor as you love yourself. Love is the key!

Chapter Twelve

What Do You Say?

A Special Request for Feedback from the Reader!

I asked youths ranging from age 12 to 26 the following question as a means of getting feedback from the younger generation:

What should adults be doing now to make the world better for upcoming generations?

Layla, age 5, says *"Play with your kids."*

C. Roper, a 22-year-old young man of North East Ohio, stated that we should *"Stop abusing the systems that we have just to get ahead so us kids can have funds when we get older. And stop letting stepparents and parents get a hold of our info and use it for their credit, for by the time we are old enough to get credit it is already bad."*

What an indictment against parents and other custodial adults. In my personal opinion this is a well-founded criticism. I have seen parents put their utilities in their child's name once the bill has become too excessive for the parents to pay in their own name. Ultimately utilities get turned off and the child's name is exploited to have service restored. Hey everybody! Stop it!

Craig, a young man of 26 told me that there is nothing the baby boomers can do outside of collaborating with youth to prevent the generation coming behind them from making the same type of decisions our generation made — which left them in such a crisis!

Maranda, age 8, says *"Surprise kids with gifts."*

I asked a young white female in Wal-Mart about this issue. The young person I asked looked approximately 17 years old. She was with her mother who would not allow the youth to answer my question. Interesting!

Jessica, a youth from San Francisco, California, told me that youth must be allowed to think for themselves without having their opinions squashed by adults. Youth should be heard and validated.

Jalen, age 12, said *"Raise your kids well."*

Drew, a young man of 24 from Chicago, stated that it was not necessarily accurate that youth are lost or floundering, but that they have found their voice, but many in the over 40 generation cannot or do not want to hear what young people have to say.

Timmy, age 16, says that *"Things are good now, why change anything?"*

Drema, age 22, told me that *"If old people can be more generous and stop being so tight with giving us money to do some of the things we like to do more often then we won't have to get involve with outside things to get money so much."*

DreShawn, age 14, replied that adults are nice, most of them, but he added, *"They try to make us believe in stuff that they believe just because they believe something don't mean that is* *right or it's what I believe. I should be able to make up my own mind."*

Aries, age 19, said, *"This mass shooting stuff got to stop! It makes me feel like not going nowhere. And all this terrorism is crazy, what wrong with yall? Stop it."*

Mike, age 10, told me, *"Get better teachers in my school."*

Now Its Your Turn!

If you are under the age of 24 and would like to join this conversation, please answer the below question, or just add your opinion or make any constructive comment and send it to the author via the below email address:

trailblazerbook@gmail.com

The question the author would like the reader to answer is as follows: *"What can the over 40 generation do now to make the world a better place for you when you are over 40?"*

About The Author

Trillazan grew up in North East Ohio. He is the son of a hardworking father who labored tirelessly on low paying jobs to provide for his family. His father purchased a home for his family to live in during the turbulent 1960s, and he demonstrated the virtue of hard work and perseverance. Trillazan's mother was an evangelical preacher who carried him to church from the time he was born. There he acquired the Godly principals that would set the tone for the remainder of his life.

Trillazan is a college graduate in the school of social work; moreover, a graduate of the school of hard knocks. The author of this book has had life experiences that prepared and qualified him as an authority on the topics of family, societal norms, religious customs and racial dysfunction. He has served the community as a teacher of youths in both public and private school systems.

The author served as a supervisor in drug and alcohol rehabilitation units, and as a health educator and community organizer in several counties in Ohio. The author assisted in the creation of the State of Ohio Clean Indoor Air Ordinance, and worked for the U.S. Justice Department Weed and Seed Program where he functioned alongside law enforcement, clergy, political, business, education and grassroots segments of society.

He toured nationally as a cast member of stage productions where he appeared on TV, radio, and stages across the country. As the leader of his own band, he pleased crowds everywhere with his silky smooth voice.

Trillazan has gained a wealth of experience dealing with the community on every level, which has positioned him perfectly as a voice for family and community reform.

References

Chapter Two: Education Is Key

1. "7 Startling Facts: An Up Close Look at Church Attendance in America," by Kelly Shattuck, December 29, 2015.
   http://churchleaders.com/pastors/pastorarticles/139575-7-startling-facts-an-up-close-look-atchurch-attendance-in-america.html

Chapter Three: The Youth Crime Paradigm

1. "Education Against Crime," by J. Edgar Hoover. In *Vital Speeches of the Day*, pp 109-113. December 1, 1936. Copyright 2003 EBSCO Publishing.
   http://connection.ebscohost.com/c/speeches/9533718/education-against-crime

2. "U.S. Single Parent Households," U.S. Census Bureau data.
   http://lib.post.ca.gov/Publications/Building%20a%20Career%20Pipeline%20Documents/Safe_Harbor.pdf

3. "U.S. Single Parent Households," Single Parent Success Foundation data.
   http://lib.post.ca.gov/Publications/Building%20a%20Career%20Pipeline%20Documents/Safe_Harbor.pdf

4. "America's Families and Living Arrangements: 2011." United States Census Bureau.
   https://www.census.gov/population/www/socdemo/hhfam/cps2011.html

5. "U.S. Single Parent Households," U.S. Census Bureau data. http://lib.post.ca.gov/Publications/Building%20a%20Career%20Pipeline%20Documents/Safe_Harbor.pdf

Chapter Four: The Sexuality Reality

1. "Does Child Abuse Cause Crime?" National Bureau of Economic Research, http://www.nber.org/digest/jan07/w12171.html

2. "Reproductive Health: Teen Pregnancy," Centers For Disease Control and Prevention. https://www.cdc.gov/teenpregnancy/about/index.htm

Chapter Five: On The Record

1. Quotes Daddy. All Quotes by George Wallace. https://www.quotesdaddy.com/author/George+Wallace

2. ThinkExist.com. Finding Quotations Was Never This Easy! David Duke Quotes. http://en.thinkexist.com/quotes/david_duke/

3. Brainyquotes.com. Benjamin Spock Quotes. https://www.brainyquote.com/quotes/authors/b/benjamin_spock.html

4. Allwords.com. McCarthyism. https://www.allwords.com/Dictionaries.php

Chapter Seven: Responsible Leadership

1. "Divorce Statistics and Divorce Rate in the USA." Divorcestatistics.info.
2. http://www.divorcestatistics.info/divorce-statistics-anddivorce-rate-in-the-usa.html

Chapter Eight: Politics And Business Leaders

1. "Prisoners in 2014," Summary, NCJ 248955, September 2015. Bureau of Justice Statistics. https://www.bjs.gov/content/pub/pdf/p14_Summary.pdf

2. *The Washington Post,* "The U.S. Has More Jails Than Colleges. Here's A Map Of Where Those Prisoners Live," by Christopher Ingraham, January 16, 2015. https://www.washingtonpost.com/news/wonk/wp/2015/01/06/the-u-s-has-more-jails-than-colleges-heres-amap-of-where-those-prisonerslive/?utm_term=.bf085ad25937

3. National Defense Budget Estimates for Fiscal Year 2015. Office of the Under Secretary of Defense (Comptroller) April, 2014. http://comptroller.defense.gov/Portals/45/Documents/defbudget/fy2015/FY15_Green_Book.pdf

Chapter Nine: The Appeal

1. "Teen Suicide Rate: Highest Increase In 15 Years." September 8, 2007. Report based on Center for Disease Control and Prevention data. https://www.sciencedaily.com/releases/2007/09/070907221530.htm